CHILD STARS

CONTENTS

50 Drew Barrymore with director Steven Spielberg on the set of 1982's *E.T.*

88 Shall we dance? *Saved by the Bell's* Elizabeth Berkley and Mario Lopez.

79 *Jerry Maguire's* Jonathan Lipnicki is still in the game

84 Bill Cosby with his huggable costar Keshia Knight Pulliam.

72
Through the magic of movies, Lindsay Lohan plays opposite herself in 1998's *The Parent Trap*.

The first thing you notice, if you're writing a book about child stars, is their sheer number: *Child Stars: Then and Now*, which focuses on kids who made it big in the '80s and '90s, includes more than 125. The second surprise is how few of them, in the modern world, really disappear: In a universe of blogs, MySpace, reality TV, direct-to-video movies, fan fairs and VH1, even those no longer in the spotlight are seldom completely off the pop-culture radar.

Child Stars offers a chance to catch up, via then-and-now photos and brief profiles, with big stars (like Drew Barrymore and Jodie Foster, who started famous and stayed that way), performers who've stayed in the business with widely varying degrees of success (more than 40, from *Boy Meets World*, *Saved by the Bell*, *Family Matters* and other shows), and kids who've gone on to build showbiz careers away from the cameras (Jeff Cohen, Chunk from *The Goonies*, is now a Hollywood lawyer). Some have found trouble, a few have died, many are happily married and raising kids of their own.

To find out who's now a chef, who married a British lord with his own splendid castle, who's making vegan cheese, who joined the circus and which former teen dreamboat has a penchant for nudism . . . turn the page.

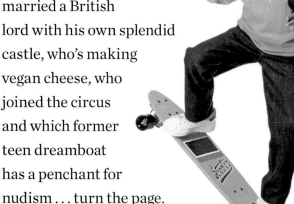

When dreamboats grow up

At their teen-heartthrob peak, they were the *Tiger Beat* boys, the stuff of tween girls' dreams, T-shirts, posters and lunch boxes. So what happened when they grew up? Turn the page . . .

→

SEE CHRIS TODAY!

A racy tale of young love, *The Blue Lagoon* made unknown Atkins, with Brooke Shields, an idol.

BLUE LAGOON

THEN Christopher Atkins never meant to burst into acting or Hollywood. "I fell in," he says. A teen model from the suburb of Rye, N.Y., he hadn't done a single audition when he got the casting call that led to his infamous sandy romp with 15-year-old Brooke Shields in 1980's *The Blue Lagoon.* He landed the role over 4,000 other hopefuls. "I'd never acted before in my life; I didn't even know what a camera looked like."

No matter. *Lagoon* was one of the biggest box office hits that year. "The movie came out, and my whole life changed," says Atkins. "There wasn't a corner on this planet that I could go where I wouldn't get mobbed."

CHRISTOPHER ATKINS

"**Everybody was running around naked,**" **Atkins says of the** *Lagoon* **shoot.** "**I got so used to it, I can't put on clothes anymore**"

Atkins relied on friends to keep him grounded and came out of the teen-idol hysteria relatively unscathed, he says. Having protective parents helped too. "They wouldn't let me buy into anything," he says. But those years weren't entirely innocent, either. "When you're 18 and the world is wild and crazy, you jump in with both feet," admits Atkins. He partied at Studio 54 and traveled the world, and he wouldn't change a thing today, he says—even if he wishes his memories were a little sharper. "I want to relive the '80s, only this time remember them," he says. "Most people out of the '80s, they either went to rehab or they died." Atkins says he realized things had gone too far when a crooked business manager left him nearly broke, and his drinking became a problem. He checked himself into rehab and has been sober for 21 years.

NOW These days he devotes his time to being a dad and a dizzying array of business ventures. "I always wanted kids," says Atkins, 47, who was married for 18 years to Australian model and *Playboy* centerfold Lynne Barron—they divorced in 2003—and has two children: Grant, 22, a baseball player at the University of North Carolina, Charlotte, and Brittney, a 21-year-old film student. "I never wanted to be one of these dads who looked over his shoulder and said, 'I wish I threw a ball to my son. I wish I read a book to my daughter,'" Atkins says. "I didn't want to miss a minute." And he didn't. "I was the baseball coach. I drove them back and forth to school, plays, birthday parties. There wasn't a place I went without them."

Lagoon has remained the zenith of Atkins' movie career. But the bronzed former idol doesn't stand idle. A fan of nudism since his days on *Lagoon*, he has posed for *Playgirl*, coaches junior high school baseball and designs and builds luxury backyard and pool environments. In his spare time, he digs for gold—literally. "It's me and four other rednecks," Atkins says of mining with pals in North Carolina. "We're like the Beverly Hillbillies." An environmentalist, he works with his uncle on developing deep-ocean pumps to protect fish and coral reefs. "I'm out there in my supercape," he jokes, "saving the world."

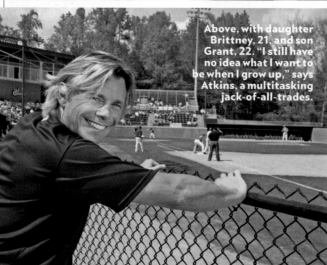

Above, with daughter Brittney, 21, and son Grant, 22. "I still have no idea what I want to be when I grow up," says Atkins, a multitasking jack-of-all-trades.

"If you've got stories, you've had adventures, and if you've had adventures, you've lived a life"

Legions of girls had crushes on Cameron as *Growing Pains'* lovable rascal Mike. But costar-turned-wife Chelsea Noble captured his heart.

KIRK CAMERON

THEN Growing up on *Growing Pains* as clown Mike Seaver, Kirk Cameron grew accustomed to seeing his signature smirk splashed across the covers of magazines like *Teen Beat* and *BOP*. "I was 15 and getting 10,000 fan letters a week, making all this money, being a teen heartthrob," recalls Cameron. "But at the same time, I was being stalked by child molesters, my parents were going through a divorce, I was an atheist. I was trying to figure out who I was."

NOW A typical Hollywood story—with a surprise twist. The only boy in a family of four kids, Cameron was all of nine when his mom trooped him and his three

sisters to meet a talent agent. A natural ham, he quickly landed a commercial for Count Chocula cereal. Other bit parts followed before he hit it big on *Growing Pains*. "People would stop me on the street sometimes, and I'd think, 'Why are they asking for my autograph? I'm not famous,'" he says, still a bit incredulous. "All of a sudden there were pillow cases and posters with my face on them. The world saw me as some kind of celebrity, but for me, life was just work and home."

At 18, he had an epiphany that abruptly changed the course of his life. "When people come up to you thinking you're a character and climbing all over you to get your

STILL GROWING

kirk
cameron

Cameron says his
bio *Still Growing*
has "all the stuff
no one knows."
Above, *Fireproof.*

autograph, it can feel kind of empty inside," he says. "I was on a hit TV show, I was making a lot of money. But I started asking myself the big questions: 'Where do we come from? Why am I here? What am I living for?'"

Cameron turned to Christianity for the answers, and never looked back. "It really had a transforming effect on my life," he says.

Since 2003 he has coproduced and starred in the syndicated Christian radio and TV talk show *The Way of the Master*, which airs two hours a day on more than 20 channels. "It's a way to say, 'Hey, I understand where you're coming from, but think about this, or think about that," says Cameron, who also writes spiritual essays for WayoftheMaster.com. "It's meant to provoke discussion."

It's not the only thing keeping him busy. Wed since 1991 to actress Chelsea Noble, he's now a proud father of six, four of them adopted, "Our life centers around the kids," says Cameron, now 37, who still calls L.A.

home. "We're very involved in their school and our church." And if he has his way, none of the children will follow his path into acting. "I wouldn't put my kids in the business. I think this industry is a really difficult, twisted place for kids to grow up," says Cameron. "The pressures are so strong, it's really easy to get messed up."

At the same time, he's grateful that it's a path that worked for him. "Knowing what I know now, I would do this again." says Cameron, who's got a romantic drama, *Fireproof,* hitting theaters this fall. "*Growing Pains* opened up doors to incredible worlds of fun and opportunity for me. If it weren't for the show, I wouldn't have met Chelsea, which means I wouldn't have my kids. My entire life would be different without it. And I love my life. So I would go back and do it again in a heartbeat." He relived the experience in his recently released memoir, *Still Growing: An Autobiography.* "I wasn't the guy in the teen mags, I was a real person."

THE NEVERENDING STORY

NOAH HATHAWAY

THEN After appearing on TV's original *Battlestar Galactica*, his portrayal of fearless kid warrior Atreyu in 1984's fantasy quest *The NeverEnding Story* led to his heartthrob status. The popular film spawned two sequels and an animated series.

NOW Venturing back into acting after raising a family, Hathaway was a production assistant, a mortgage broker and a bartender. He's getting ready for a big-budget remake of his 1986 cult classic *Troll*. "I'm going to play the evil wizard this time," says Hathaway, 36. "He's a crazy warrior."

HOME IMPROVEMENT

JONATHAN TAYLOR THOMAS

THEN Best known as the smart-mouthed middle son, Randy, on the ABC sitcom *Home Improvement*, Thomas also succeeded off-camera as the voice of Young Simba in Disney's animated feature *The Lion King*.
NOW After appearances on series such as *Smallville*, *Veronica Mars* and *Ally McBeal*, Thomas enrolled at Columbia University.

JOSEPH GORDON-LEVITT

THEN Aliens' son Tommy Solomon on NBC's *3rd Rock from the Sun*.

NOW Since *3rd Rock* went off the air in 2001, Gordon-Levitt, 27, has kept at least a big toe in the Hollywood pool—and, more recently, has had the opportunity to jump in head first, twice. The actor, who got his start in Cocoa Puffs and Pop-Tarts commercials, worked in independent films like 2004's *Mysterious Skin*, in which he played a gay prostitute, and 2005's *Brick*, a dark film about drugs and murder at a high school. More recently, he costarred opposite Ryan Phillippe in *Stop-Loss*, about the emotional toll paid by American soldiers stationed in Iraq. Next year, as the Cobra Commander, he'll confront the fantasy forces of all things right and good in *G.I. Joe*.

"I was the golden boy. It was this idealized version of me"

CHAD ALLEN

THEN Child actor on *St. Elsewhere* and later a teen star on *Dr. Quinn, Medicine Woman*; fan magazines proclaiming him a clean-cut good guy confound Chad Allen to this day. "I was the golden boy," he says. "It was this idealized version of me, so far removed from my reality. I had no idea who that kid was." **NOW** A huge life change. The youngest of six kids, Chad Allen Lazzari and his twin sister, Charity, grew up in a strict Catholic family in Long Beach, Calif. The kids scored their first gig, a McDonald's commercial, when they were 4. Charity quit acting a few years later, but Chad continued to land a growing string of roles on *Webster, Our House* and *St. Elsewhere*. By 14, he was a regular on *My Two Dads*. At some point it began to feel like work. "It changed from just being fun to making enough money to support a lot of people," he says.

Disenchanted, Allen quit the business at 16 to return to school full-time. Ironically, "that's where I fell in love with acting," he says. "I fell in with the theater kids, so I was having fun doing plays."

Focused on a theater career, Allen was accepted at New York University but put college on hold when he landed *Dr. Quinn*. "I thought I could shoot the pilot, then head off to school," says Allen, whose five years as the show's do-gooder Matthew Cooper cemented his squeaky-clean status.

Then came the moment: In 1996 Allen was outed by a tabloid that published a photo of him kissing another man. "It was sold to them by [an] ex," he says. "The publicists were like, 'We can fix this. We can get you a girlfriend.' But I didn't want to do that. I was tired of lying." So, he notes, "I didn't get another network audition for years after that." Eventually, he came out publicly on his own.

Allen recently relived the dilemma in Hartford, Conn., in the Tony-nominated production *The Little Dog Laughed*. "It's such a familiar story to me," says Allen of the play, which focuses on a big-name actor deciding to go public about his homosexuality. "But I think we're at the stage now that we should be able to focus on telling stories about interesting characters who happen to be gay."

Case in point: Allen's series of made-for-TV films about private eye Donald Strachey for gay network Here TV. "He's just a quirky P.I. who happens to be in a very loving relationship with his boyfriend."

Now living in L.A. with his partner of three years and their dog, Foxy Brown, Allen, now 34, took on his biggest role starring in and producing *Save Me*, a dark comedy about born-again heterosexuals that premiered at Sundance last year. He also keeps busy working with LGBT nonprofits and often spends time with gay teens who feel the need to talk. "I still get so much mail, and I really do try to reach out," he says. "I've been in that place. The depression, the drugs: It's so important to be able to connect with someone. I didn't have that kind of role model to turn to when I was growing up. So I made a decision to be who I am and not hide it."

In *My Two Dads*, Allen (right) costarred with Giovanni Ribisi and Stacy Keanan.

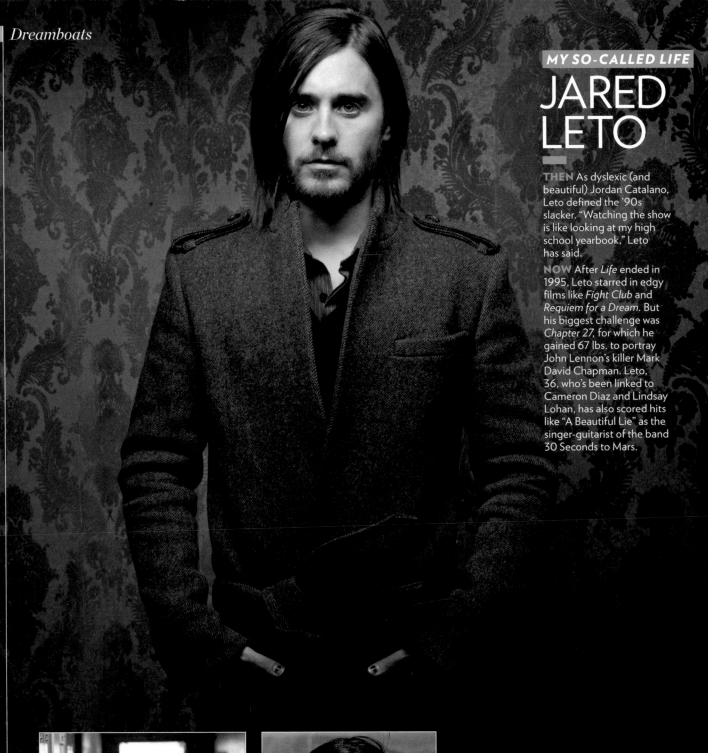

Dreamboats

MY SO-CALLED LIFE

JARED LETO

THEN As dyslexic (and beautiful) Jordan Catalano, Leto defined the '90s slacker. "Watching the show is like looking at my high school yearbook," Leto has said.

NOW After *Life* ended in 1995, Leto starred in edgy films like *Fight Club* and *Requiem for a Dream*. But his biggest challenge was *Chapter 27*, for which he gained 67 lbs. to portray John Lennon's killer Mark David Chapman. Leto, 36, who's been linked to Cameron Diaz and Lindsay Lohan, has also scored hits like "A Beautiful Lie" as the singer-guitarist of the band 30 Seconds to Mars.

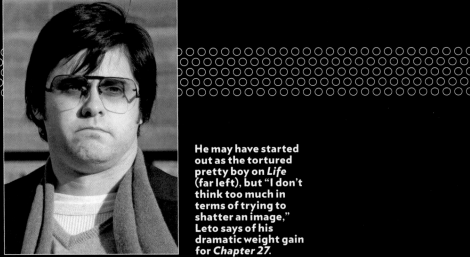

He may have started out as the tortured pretty boy on *Life* (far left), but "I don't think too much in terms of trying to shatter an image," Leto says of his dramatic weight gain for *Chapter 27*.

JOEY LAWRENCE

THEN Though the girls noticed his good looks as a child star in *Gimme a Break!*, they really paid attention when Lawrence became a teen heartthrob in *Blossom*, complete with his own catchphrase: "Whoa!"

NOW Lawrence, 32, goes by Joseph now. He has recently appeared as Clay Dobson on the CBS drama *CSI: NY* and starred on Broadway as Billy Flynn in the long-running hit *Chicago*. He also got a sudden, surprise career boost when he showed off his moves—and his newly shaved head—on *Dancing with the Stars*. He and wife Chandie had a daughter, Charli, in 2006.

Lawrence made his mark playing a pair of Joeys: He was Joey Donovan in *Gimme a Break!* before blossoming into Joey Russo in *Blossom*.

"I became an adult before I had a kid, which I highly recommend," Bateman told PEOPLE following the birth of his daughter.

LITTLE HOUSE ON THE PRAIRIE

JASON BATEMAN

THEN In 1981 Bateman—brother of sitcom star Justine Bateman—portrayed innocent James Cooper Ingalls for 21 episodes of the television drama *Little House on the Prairie,* followed by two seasons playing wiseacre Derek Taylor, Ricky Schroder's best friend in *Silver Spoons.*

NOW Following a stint on TV's *Arrested Development,* Bateman, now 39, charmed as the adoptive father in *Juno.* In real life, he's married to Paul Anka's daughter Amanda; they have a daughter, Francesca Nora Bateman, 19 months.

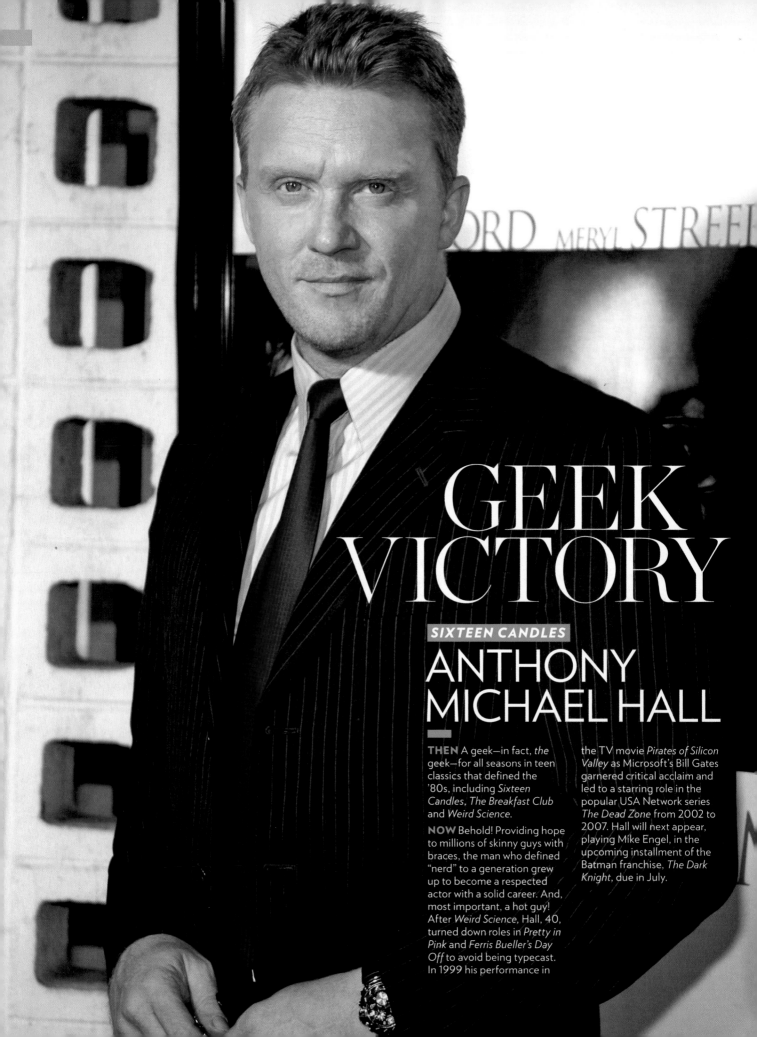

GEEK VICTORY

ANTHONY MICHAEL HALL

THEN A geek—in fact, *the* geek—for all seasons in teen classics that defined the '80s, including *Sixteen Candles*, *The Breakfast Club* and *Weird Science*.

NOW Behold! Providing hope to millions of skinny guys with braces, the man who defined "nerd" to a generation grew up to become a respected actor with a solid career. And, most important, a hot guy! After *Weird Science*, Hall, 40, turned down roles in *Pretty in Pink* and *Ferris Bueller's Day Off* to avoid being typecast. In 1999 his performance in the TV movie *Pirates of Silicon Valley* as Microsoft's Bill Gates garnered critical acclaim and led to a starring role in the popular USA Network series *The Dead Zone* from 2002 to 2007. Hall will next appear, playing Mike Engel, in the upcoming installment of the Batman franchise, *The Dark Knight*, due in July.

Who would have thought this nerdy-looking youth would grow up to be a handsome young man?

GEEK VICTORY

STAND BY ME
JERRY O'CONNELL

THEN In 1986's *Stand By Me*, he played Vern Tessio—overweight, shy and often bullied.

NOW Slim, trim and showcasing his comedic chops. In 2008 O'Connell earned laughs with a dead-on Tom Cruise impression in a skit on Will Ferrell's humor Web site FunnyorDie.com. This fall he will appear in a new sitcom on Fox called *Do Not Disturb*, the pilot for which was directed by fellow former child actor Jason Bateman. On July 14, 2007, he married actress and former model Rebecca Romijn (above).

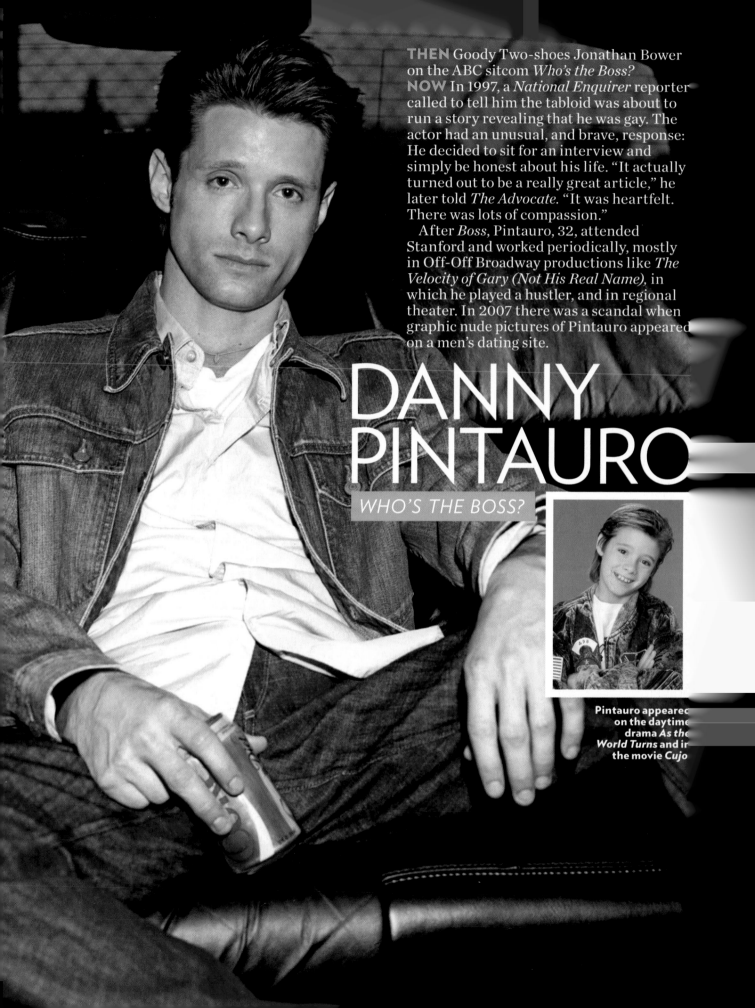

THEN Goody Two-shoes Jonathan Bower on the ABC sitcom *Who's the Boss?*
NOW In 1997, a *National Enquirer* reporter called to tell him the tabloid was about to run a story revealing that he was gay. The actor had an unusual, and brave, response: He decided to sit for an interview and simply be honest about his life. "It actually turned out to be a really great article," he later told *The Advocate*. "It was heartfelt. There was lots of compassion."

After *Boss*, Pintauro, 32, attended Stanford and worked periodically, mostly in Off-Off Broadway productions like *The Velocity of Gary (Not His Real Name)*, in which he played a hustler, and in regional theater. In 2007 there was a scandal when graphic nude pictures of Pintauro appeared on a men's dating site.

DANNY PINTAURO

WHO'S THE BOSS?

Pintauro appeared on the daytime drama *As the World Turns* and in the movie *Cujo*

Second Life

Medieval literature professor? Brain chemistry researcher? Veterinarian? Vegan-cheese whiz? Some of them still perform a bit, but for the most part these former child stars all found a new—and often surprising—second act

SEE
DANICA
TODAY!

*Savage passion!: As
brainy Winnie Cooper,
Danica McKellar played
puppy-love interest to
The Wonder Years' Kevin
Arnold (Fred Savage).*

THE WONDER YEARS
DANICA McKELLAR

THEN Winnie Cooper, the object of affection for Fred Savage's character, Kevin Arnold.

NOW McKellar, 33, still acts but has made a bigger impact off-screen. While earning a degree in mathematics from UCLA she coauthored a paper, "Percolation and Gibbs States Multiplicity for Ferromagnetic Ashkin-Teller Models on Z^2," in the prestigious *Journal of Physics A: Mathematical and General*. On television, McKellar has a recurring role in the CBS sitcom *How I Met Your Mother*.

Last year McKellar published *Math Doesn't Suck*, aimed at making math more interesting to teenage girls. Her next, *Kiss My Math*, is due in August.

WILLY WONKA &
THE CHOCOLATE FACTORY

PETER OSTRUM

THEN Charlie Bucket, the kid at the heart of the original *Willy Wonka & the Chocolate Factory* (1971).

NOW A large-animal veterinarian and father of two in upstate New York. Ostrum, 50, didn't have a passion for acting and rarely talks about the movie, except to elementary school kids. During an NPR interview in connection with the Johnny Depp version of the film released in 2005, Ostrum's wife, Loretta, 55, recalled that when they were dating he didn't mention *Wonka* until she was about to meet his mother. "He says, 'Oh, in case someone brings it up, I was once in this movie.' [He] said, you know, *Willy Wonka,'*" she said. "And I just thought, 'Oh,' because I'd never seen it. So I didn't think too much of it."

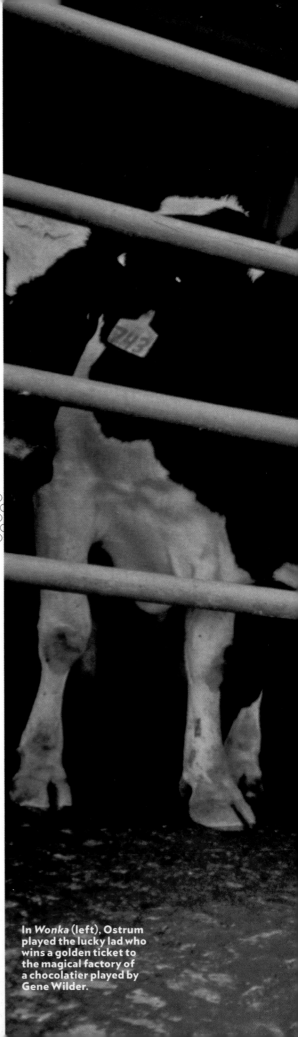

In *Wonka* (left), Ostrum played the lucky lad who wins a golden ticket to the magical factory of a chocolatier played by Gene Wilder.

66 **I had fun making the movie but I wasn't convinced acting was what I wanted to do**

Jeremy: forever famous for his trademark "Ben Seaver scream" on *Growing Pains*.

GROWING PAINS
JEREMY MILLER

THEN Huggable little brother Ben Seaver on *Growing Pains* for seven seasons.

NOW After *Pains* wrapped in 1992, Miller, 31, had to sow a few oats. "For about two years, I was a little wild. I was out partying, having adventures," Miller told PEOPLE in 2000. He tried college at USC, dropping out after a year because of attention deficit disorder. But Miller, whose grandmother was a chef and taught him a love of cooking, found his niche in culinary school and soon opened his own catering business in L.A. The *other*

biz still beckoned, however—at least in China, where *Pains* was one of the few American shows broadcast during the '80s and earned a huge following. Miller starred in a film that opened in Shanghai this year and told Larry King he's trying to develop a cooking show for Chinese audiences. He's also made a foray into the food world with a distinctly American flavor: a recent commercial for McDonald's.

THE BRADY BUNCH
EVE PLUMB

THEN Jan, the iconically overshadowed middle child from the famous '70s sitcom.
NOW On the *Brady* set, "we would always have little art shows," says Plumb, 50. "I kept working at it until I had the confidence to put something up on the wall." Married in 1995 to computer analyst Ken Pace, the Laguna Beach, Calif., artist's oil paintings fetch up to $5,000 at galleries nationwide. "If I hadn't seen all that rejection as an actor, this would be difficult," says Plumb, who still has a thing for acting. "I would love to do television again. It's where I grew up, where I'm comfortable."

"I have about three pieces going at a time," says Plumb of her artwork.

Top to bottom: With BB, Lilly, Reggie and Deuce; *A Christmas Story*; and *The Toy*.

SCOTT SCHWARTZ

THEN Disenchanted rich kid Eric Bates in *The Toy* with Richard Pryor, and Flick, infamous victim of an ill-fated flagpole experiment in *A Christmas Story*. "[It's] ironic a nice Jewish kid from Jersey would be in two Christmas movies," Schwartz says of his two most memorable roles. He was 13 when he filmed *Story*.

NOW At 31, he's a product specialist for Donruss Trading Cards, where he relies on his energetic personality to get celeb pals to sign autographs. "I've been bright and bubbly since I can remember," he says. The world of trading cards and collectibles is now old hat to Schwartz, since he and his father have run a sports and movie memorabilia store in Westlake Village, Calif., for the past 21 years. Schwartz is grateful for his colorful life experiences—even his stint working in the adult film industry, which he calls "a little blip" in the grand scheme of things. "I have no ego to bruise," he says.

KELLIE WILLIAMS

THEN Laura Winslow, the straitlaced, unwilling object of nerd Steve Urkel's desire. "We were really like family," she says of her 9 years on the show. "Everything that people saw was real, at least to me."

NOW Founded and runs Kellie Williams Programs, a DC-based after-school arts program designed for young people to gain exposure to theater, music, visual arts and dance. Williams' inspiration stems from her own experience at an early age. "I think young people can make better choices when they are exposed to different environments," she says. The ambitious 32-year-old started the program (more info is available at kelliewilliamsprograms .com) in 2004 with her own money but has since drummed up support from the D.C. city council and generous contributions from local professionals. Willams says her biggest payoff is the pride she feels from her students' accomplishments.

"It feels good," Williams says of her current gig.

35

HONEY, I SHRUNK THE KIDS

AMY O'NEILL

THEN Anxious older sis Amy Szalinski in Disney's '89 blockbuster. O'Neill says working on the backyard-on-steroids set "made you feel like you were in another dimension."

NOW A performance artist who specializes in circus art and miming. "Growing up, I had practiced improvisation in the style of *commedia dell'arte*, which uses a lot of circus skills," she says of her roots. "I fell in love with performing." O'Neill crafts each show from scratch, drawing on a bag of tricks that includes juggling swords and walking on a ball in high heels. She teaches circus arts at L.A.'s Hope Street Family Center and performs with a tap-dancing troupe. Her shows have taken her all over the world, including to Abu Dhabi in 2007. "I never know what to expect," she says. "That's part of the thrill of this lifestyle."

O'Neill with
Honey costar
Thomas Wilson
Brown and, above,
working her big-
top magic.

"I want to raise the next generation of activists," says Frye (with Goldberg and daughters Poet and Jagger).

PUNKY BREWSTER

SOLEIL MOON FRYE

THEN At 8, she was spunky Punky Brewster on the kids' comedy. Says Frye: "NBC was our playground."
NOW A married mom of two daughters, Poet, 2, and Jagger, 3 months, Frye just opened the Little Seed, an environmentally conscious baby shop. (Dad is Ashton Kutcher's producing partner Jason Goldberg.) "When I had Poet, it was like my eyes were opened up for the first time," says Frye, 31. "Little Seed was born from my girlfriends and I having kids and searching for alternatives for our children that were healthy and organic and nontoxic." Frye is also digging into her roots, producing *Sonny Boy*, which won best documentary at the San Diego Film Festival, about her dad, Virgil Frye, a former boxing champ and civil rights activist. "My father has Alzheimer's, and before it's too late we decided to trace his history," she says. "We jumped in an RV and did a road trip from L.A. back to Iowa. It was a real bonding experience for us."

BLOSSOM

MAYIM BIALIK

THEN Best remembered as the hat-loving title character on NBC's *Blossom*.

NOW She hit the books—hard—earning her Ph.D. in neuroscience at UCLA last year. "My thesis has a long, pretentious-looking title," says Bialik, 32. "But my field is psychoneuroendocrinology, studying OCD behaviors in individuals with Prader-Willi syndrome," which causes developmental delays. While she still reviews grants, Bialik segued back into acting with roles as a lesbian on *Curb Your Enthusiasm* and as a much crankier version of herself on *Fat Actress*. This fall she's expecting her second child with grad-student husband Michael Stone. "I'm working overtime being a mom," says Bialik. "But I'd love to do a sitcom again. I'm curious to see if I'm the kind of child actor who can make it as an adult."

"Hollywood is a hard world for grown-ups, so it's a really hard world for a kid," says Bialik. "Rejection was very difficult. It still is."

"It was good to kiss Kelly LeBrock for a day," he says about that famous make-out scene.

ILAN MITCHELL-SMITH

" I like empowering students"

THEN Endearing computer geek Wyatt in the 1985 hit *Weird Science*. "It was really luck—luck that I was happy people mistook for skill," Smith says about his acting career.
NOW *Doctor* Mitchell-Smith: With a Ph.D. in medieval English literature, he is a professor at Angelo State University in San Angelo Texas. "I grew up the biggest *Dungeons & Dragons* nerd," says Mitchell-Smith, 39, who these days indulges his Gothic interests at the office. He's currently at work on his latest treatise, *Between Mars and Venus: Balance and Excess in Chivalry in the Late Medieval English Period*. Though his Hollywood career is long over, Mitchell-Smith still gets recognized. Recently, a group of his students gave a presentation on popular culture and "without telling me first," he says, "they showed a clip of *Weird Science*." On the home front, Mitchell-Smith enjoys "special meals" with his family, particularly when they include his wife Susannah's treats. "She teaches [the kids] to bake and I get to eat it," he says. With daughter Eloise, 9, and son Asher, 7, he likes to play kid-friendly card games. "We've been doing a lot of Pokémon," he says.

41

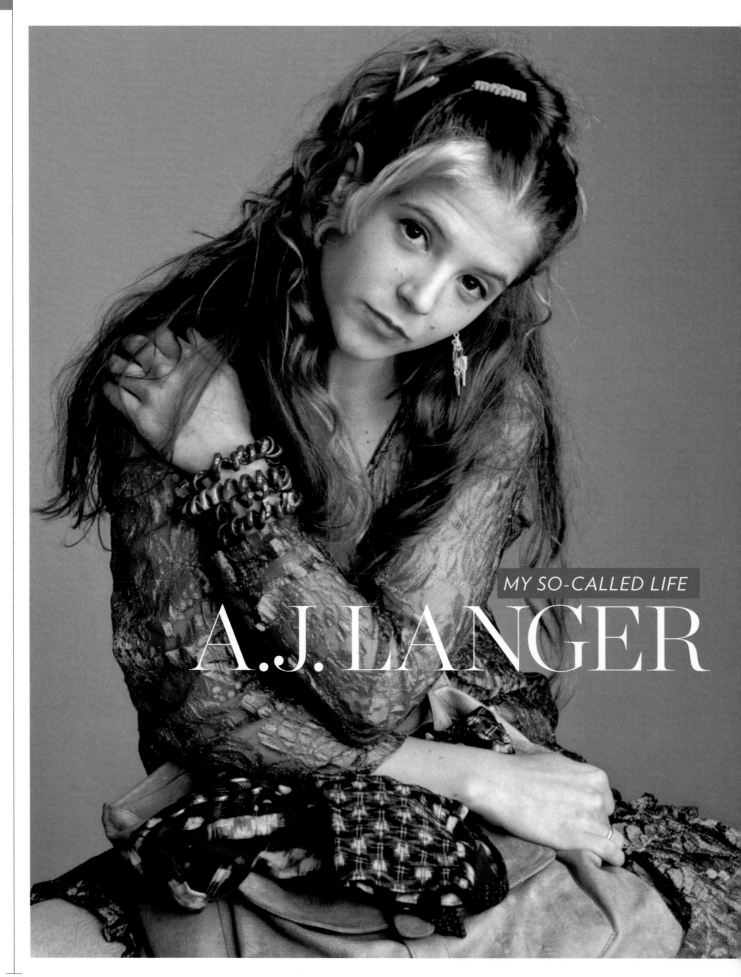

MY SO-CALLED LIFE

A.J. LANGER

"It's out of a fairy tale," says Langer of England's Powderham Castle, which she and husband Courtenay (with baby Joscelyn, below) plan to call home someday.

THEN Bad girl Rayanne Graff on *My So-Called Life*. "Rayanne's like a friend who's always there," says Langer. "That show had magic from day one."

NOW So how did Langer meet her husband, Charlie Courtenay, 32, the future Earl of Devon? "We met in a bar in Vegas. He didn't know I was an actress. I didn't know he had a castle," says Langer, 34. "So we're about even." Langer and Courtenay, an L.A. lawyer, plan to eventually call the 14th-century Powderham Castle in Devon, England, home. "They do weddings and events there. It's really dramatic and really cool." In the meantime, the new mom (baby Joscelyn is 17 months) plays beach bum between gigs on TV shows like *It's Like, You Know . . .* and *Three Sisters.* "I have fibromyalgia, so on a daily basis there's always something hurting," says Langer of the chronic pain disease, diagnosed when she was 23. "Surfing and meditation help me let go of the pain. So now, the philosophy for me is work to surf."

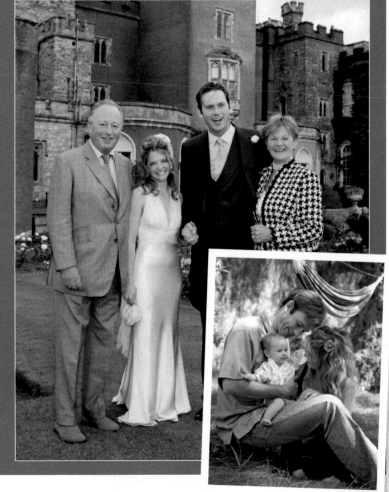

DICK TRACY
CHARLIE KORSMO

THEN Though he made a name for himself in two big-budget films, *Dick Tracy* and *Hook*, what Korsmo remembers most about those experiences isn't the glitz and glamour of working on a movie set but being away from home for six to seven months at a time. "I was only 10 when we filmed [*Tracy*]," he says. "In a peculiar way, you don't appreciate everything that's going on."

NOW Despite another scene-stealing performance in 1998's high school party comedy *Can't Hardly Wait*, Korsmo bade adieu to his acting career and returned to college at MIT. After graduation Korsmo headed to Capitol Hill armed with a physics degree, where he worked for the Environmental Protection Agency and in Congress for the Chairman of the House Policy and Homeland Security Committees. "I was the committee parliamentarian, doing a lot of the drafting a lawyer would do," he says. "I applied to law school early on after that and went straight to Yale." Korsmo is only occasionally recognized from his acting and is content to have left his career in Hollywood. "There's nothing I did that I would have done differently," he says. "It allowed me to pay for all the schooling I've had."

The recently married 29-year-old currently puts in long hours working in litigation at a corporate law firm in New York. "I'm hoping to eventually be one of those guys in the courtroom," says Korsmo. "Maybe my acting experience could help me with that."

Korsmo still keeps in touch with his *Hook* director, Steven Spielberg, through holiday cards and letters. "He's a great and warm man," Korsmo says.

Says Smith: "I want to use whatever recognition I have to do something good."

TARAN NOAH SMITH

HOME IMPROVEMENT

THEN He spent eight years as Tim Allen's youngest son, Mark, on *Home Improvement*. "By 15, I got to travel the world, make a speech on the White House lawn, fly a blimp," says Smith. "But I didn't have some very basic normal kid experiences."

NOW At 17, Smith wed 32-year-old Heidi Van Pelt. Since their 2005 split, the couple have been battling over the future of their vegan cheese company, Playfood. Still, the business is thriving, with four kinds of cashew-based cheese. "We're at the stage where it's the equivalent of a band signing to a major label," says Smith, now 24. "By this time next year we'll be everywhere." He's also turned activist, joining actress Daryl Hannah to promote her green-living site, DHLoveLife.com.

Dustin Hoffman, Meryl Streep and Henry, age 8, in 1979's Oscar-winning divorce drama, *Kramer vs. Kramer*.

KRAMER VS. KRAMER

JUSTIN HENRY

THEN The youngest actor ever nominated for an Academy Award, Henry tugged at America's heartstrings as Billy Kramer, the kid caught in a nasty custody battle in *Kramer vs. Kramer*. Five years later he was Molly Ringwald's obnoxious younger bro, Mike Baker, in *Sixteen Candles*.

NOW A business development specialist for new media. The college grad discovered his entrepreneurial edge when he and friends started the Slamdunk Film Festival in 1998, the first to exhibit movies completely digitally. By 2001, Slamdunk was turning a good profit and ready to launch a distribution label when 9/11 "took us out at the kneecaps," says Henry.

"I learned through that experience that I loved the business of producing." On the personal front, he is a divorced doting father of 2-year-old Sabine, for whom he loves playing guitar and drums. (*Kramer*'s Dustin Hoffman gave him his first drum set.) Henry still takes time for acting gigs but isn't ready to give up his day job. "Until something lines up nicely, I'm really content working in business," he says. "I love the action."

ARIANA RICHARDS

THEN Scene-stealer in creature classics *Tremors* and *Jurassic Park*.

NOW A successful painter living a "romantic life" surrounded by vineyards and horses in Oregon's Willamette Valley. "Being a painter is one of the most natural things in the world to me," Richards says, "Even as a 12-year-old, I was taking intensive tutoring from professors and learning classical methods." Maybe it's in her blood: Richards is a descendant of an Italian Renaissance artist and sold her first painting, of two golden retrievers, at 14. Now 28, she enjoys the freedom and independence the profession allows her. "I like the fact that I'm my own director," she says. She still keeps in touch with Hollywood friends: *Jurassic* director Steven Spielberg keeps one of her watercolors in his collection. "I do have a charmed life," she says. "There is a lot of variety."

Samples of Richards' art: "Lady of the Dahlias" (the "lady" is Ariana's younger sister Bethany) and, inset, "The Singing Spring."

Richards in April 2008; above, in *Jurassic* with Sam Neill, top, Laura Dern and Joseph Mazello.

Still
in the
Spotlight

Once upon a time, they were really famous. And now . . .
they're *still* famous. For the most part, you already
know their stories; here's a reminder of what they looked
like then and who they are now

SEE DREW TODAY!

In 1982's *E.T.* Drew Barrymore (as Gertie) taught an alien how to talk.

DREW BARRYMORE

THEN The precocious scion of Hollywood's Barrymore clan was all of 7 when she stole hearts in 1982's *E.T.* "One day I was a little girl, and the next day I was being mobbed by people who wanted me to sign my autograph or pose for pictures or who just wanted to touch me," she told PEOPLE in 1989. "I was this 7-year-old who was expected to be going on a mature 29."

NOW After teen battles with drugs and alcohol, a suicide attempt at 14—plus two quickie marriages and divorces—Drew cleaned up well, producing and starring in films like the *Charlie's Angels* franchise and the upcoming *He's Just Not That into You.* She met new beau Justin Long, 30, best known as the Mac guy, on the set of *Into You* last year after ending a four-year relationship with Strokes drummer Fabrizio Moretti. At 33, she says she has never been happier. "I've found a best friend," she said on *Oprah* in March. Her free-spirited philosophy? "Let your freak-flag fly," she told PEOPLE, "and if someone doesn't get you, move on."

BROOKE SHIELDS

THEN Controversy, controversy, controversy. At 12, she starred as a teen prostitute in Louis Malle's 1978 drama *Pretty Baby* and showed off more skin in 1980's steamy *Blue Lagoon*. At 14, in a famous Calvin Klein jeans commercial, she cooed, "Do you want to know what comes between me and my Calvins? Nothing." **NOW** Now 43, the Princeton grad played a hitherto unheralded flair for comedy on the NBC series *Suddenly Susan* and wrote about her battle with postpartum depression in her memoir *Down Came the Rain*, which triggered a public battle with Tom Cruise. He criticized her use of prescription drugs but later apologized. Wed to her second husband, writer Chris Henchy, since 2001, Shields now plays mom to two daughters, Rowan and Grier, when she's not on the set of NBC's drama *Lipstick Jungle*.

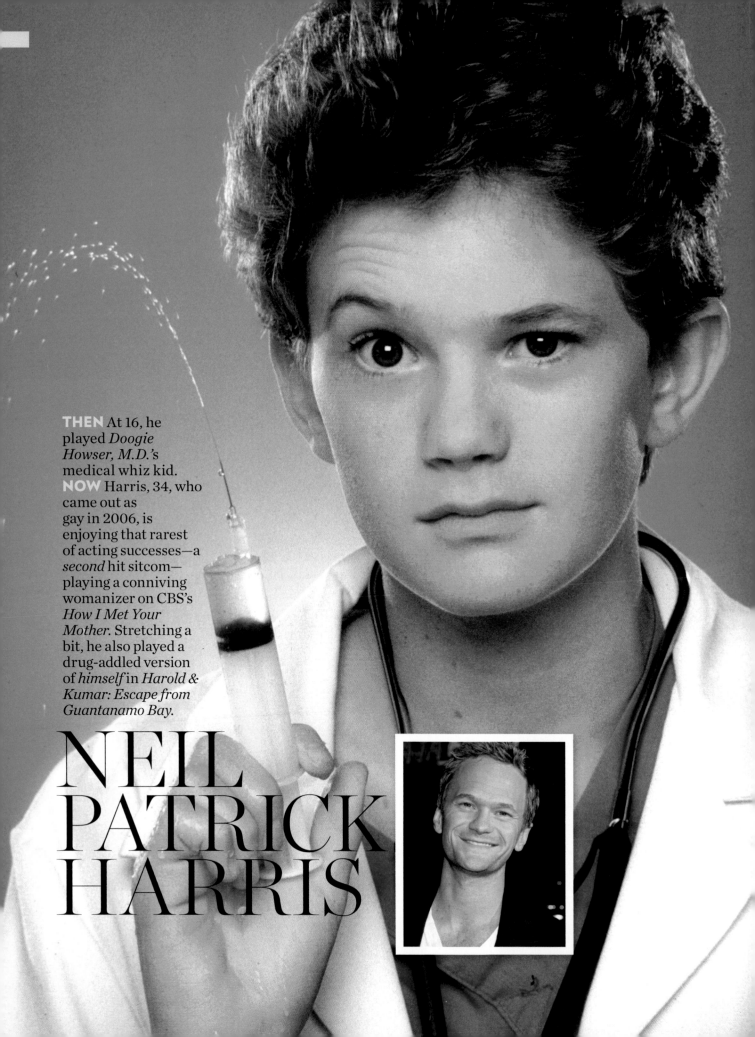

THEN At 16, he played *Doogie Howser, M.D.*'s medical whiz kid. **NOW** Harris, 34, who came out as gay in 2006, is enjoying that rarest of acting successes—a *second* hit sitcom—playing a conniving womanizer on CBS's *How I Met Your Mother.* Stretching a bit, he also played a drug-addled version of *himself* in *Harold & Kumar: Escape from Guantanamo Bay.*

NEIL PATRICK HARRIS

SARAH JESSICA PARKER

THEN At 16, she played desperate-to-fit-in brainiac Patty Greene on TV's short-lived high school comedy *Square Pegs*.
NOW Full-fledged superstar, fashion maven and designer; elevated to iconic status with her portrayal of *Sex and the City*'s chief siren and sexpert, Carrie Bradshaw.

Square Pegs Patty evolved into *Sex and the City*'s ultimate urbanite and a real-life glam mom.

The Thinking Man's Bat: In *Batman Begins*, Bale turned the cartoon hero into a complex character. Left, *The Machinist*.

CHRISTIAN BALE

THEN At 13, Bale beat out hundreds of other kids to play a young Japanese concentration camp survivor in Steven Spielberg's pre-Pearl Harbor drama *Empire of the Sun* (1987).

NOW A big screen star with epic cred and a cult following. The Welsh-born actor, 34, is known for risky roles (*American Psycho*) and radical transformation (he famously lost 63 lbs. to play a tormented insomniac in *The Machinist*, then immediately bulked up to star in *Batman Begins*). Next up for Bale is this summer's *The Dark Night*, the latest Batman fim.

KIRSTEN DUNST

THEN Sweet, ethereal 12-year-old bloodsucker in 1994's *Interview with the Vampire* (where she received her first onscreen kiss, from Brad Pitt). **NOW** Most famously, Spidey's sweetie, Mary Jane Watson, in three big-screen installments of the *Spider-Man* series. In February, a source close to the actress, who has dated Jake Gyllenhaal and been active on the L.A. party circuit, told PEOPLE that she had checked into rehab. "People were pushing her to go in there but there was no intervention," the source said. "She has been partying hard for a while, and I'm sure the Heath Ledger thing put people over the edge." Dunst, 26, has since returned to work; her upcoming films include *How to Lose Friends & Alienate People* and *All Good Things*, costarring Ryan Gosling.

AGE 13

THE PROFESSIONAL
Portman made her big-screen debut opposite an assassin-babysitter played by Jean Reno.

AGE 15

BEAUTIFUL GIRLS
Portman played Timothy Hutton's teen crush.

AGE 18

STAR WARS
As Padmé Amidala, she fought for her native Naboo.

NATALIE PORTMAN

THEN In the critically acclaimed 1994 indie film *The Professional*, Portman, 13, played an orphan who forges an unlikely friendship with an assassin.

NOW Portman, 27, has enjoyed steady success in the industry with a string of high-profile performances, including Queen Amidala in the most recent *Star Wars* trilogy; Alice, a conflicted stripper, in *Closer* (for which she won a Golden Globe); and the ambitious, ill-fated Anne Boleyn opposite Scarlett Johansson's Mary Boleyn, the younger sister, in *The Other Boleyn Girl*. The socially conscious Harvard grad recently launched a line of cruelty-free vegan footwear. Her upcoming films include *Brothers* and *New York, I Love You*.

KIDS INC.

JENNIFER LOVE HEWITT

THEN At 10, she patented that sunshiney grin on *Kids Incorporated*, then won fans as Sarah Reeves on *Party of Five* for five years.
NOW After a quickly canceled *Party* spinoff called *Time of Your Life*, Hewitt, 29, moved on to the big screen with *I Know What You Did Last Summer* and *Heartbreakers*. She also released four pop CDs before scoring a steady gig as the title character in the CBS drama *The Ghost Whisperer*. Linked in the past to *Boy Meets World*'s Will Friedle, singer Enrique Iglesias and Carson Daly, Hewitt has been engaged to Scottish actor Ross McCall since November. Despite a battle with paparazzi over some unflattering bikini photos last year, she shows off her figure—in Hanes underwear ads.

Disney Channel's hit *Kids Incorporated's* cast included pals Jennifer Love Hewitt (right) and Fergie.

FERGIE

THEN At 9, she was little Stacy Ferguson on *Kids Incorporated*.
NOW Formerly a member of the girl group Wild Orchid and the only female Black Eyed Pea, she has since moved on to a sizzling solo career, scoring chart-toppers like "London Bridge" and "Big Girls Don't Cry." Engaged to *Las Vegas* star Josh Duhamel, Fergie, 33, also appeared in 2006's *Poseidon* and fan Quentin Tarantino's latest film, *Grindhouse*.

Lane and Brolin (in L.A. in 2008) have been married for almost four years.

WHEN CHILD STARS MARRY

DIANE LANE

THEN It girl Sherri "Cherry" Valance in Francis Ford Coppola's ensemble classic *The Outsiders* (1983).

NOW Earned acclaim in 1989's TV film *Lonesome Dove.* Oscar nominee for 2002's *Unfaithful.* Lane, 43, next stars in the drama *Nights in Rodanthe* with her *Unfaithful* costar Richard Gere.

JOSH BROLIN

THEN Big brother Brand Walsh in '80s fave *The Goonies.*

NOW Since his star-making turn in 2007's *No Country for Old Men,* Brolin, 40, has seen his Hollywood stock rise. Next up are the biopics *Milk,* about assassinated gay politician Harvey Milk, and *W.,* about President Bush.

CHRISTINA RICCI

THEN Wednesday, *The Addams Family*'s morbid moppet (age 11, 1991).

NOW Producer and critically lauded indie-movie vet, recently seen in the live-action version of *Speed Racer*. The 28-year-old actress has *lots* of tattoos, including a lion on her right shoulder blade, a bluebird on her right breast, a bouquet of sweetpeas on her lower back and the words "Move or Bleed" on her rib cage.

If this is Wednesday, it must be *The Addams Family*. A newly blonde Ricci (photographed in April 2008) has lightened up considerably since she played the child of Gomez and Morticia Addams.

VALERIE BERTINELLI

THEN Perpetually perky *One Day at a Time* teen Barbara Cooper (1975, age 15). **NOW** Made-for-TV-movie staple turned confessional author, Jenny Craig spokeswoman and 40-lb.-weight-loss goddess (age 48).

Val lost **40** lbs.

BEFORE "I'm Italian—I don't have to be sad to eat or happy to eat."

Innocence, a lisp and orange hair made the Oklahoma-born Howard a standout in *The Music Man*. He got a second bite of the apple in *Happy Days* (below, with Henry Winkler) en route to becoming an Academy Award-winning director (*A Beautiful Mind*).

RON HOWARD

THEN A generation's all-American kid; charmed audiences in *The Music Man* at age 8 and, for years, as Opie on *The Andy Griffith Show*.
NOW Age 54, an Oscar-winning director, father of four and a grandfather; next up: the post-Watergate-era drama *Frost/Nixon*.

Buddy film: The friendship between Frodo (Wood) and Samwise (Astin) was at the heart of the *Rings* trilogy.

AVALON
Roger Ebert once called him "the most talented actor in his age group in Hollywood history."

THE GOONIES
Who doesn't enjoy a good yarn about pirate treasure and real estate development?

ELIJAH WOOD

THEN Doe-eyed Michael Kaye in the Oscar-nominated family drama *Avalon* (1990).

NOW In the aftermath of career-defining success as Frodo Baggins in the *Lord of the Rings*, Wood, 27, has sought to avoid typecasting: He played a serial killer in *Sin City* and voiced Mumble the penguin in *Happy Feet*.

SEAN ASTIN

THEN "Goonies never say die!": the unshakably optimistic Mikey Walsh in '80s cult classic *The Goonies* (1985).

NOW Married and a father of three girls, Astin, 37, has made his mark playing unlikely heroes: Frodo's *Rings* sidekick Samwise Gamgee and football phenom Rudy Ruettiger in *Rudy*.

THEN At 13, she scored a star turn in *The Horse Whisperer*, opposite Robert Redford.
NOW She graduated to subdued-but-sexy roles in *Lost in Translation* and *The Other Boleyn Girl*. Next up: *He's Just Not That into You*. Johansson, 23, has dated Jared Leto and Josh Hartnett and been linked to Justin Timberlake; she confirmed her engagement to actor Ryan Reynolds in May. She has also been outspoken about being sexually responsible: "I get tested for HIV twice a year. . . ." she told *Allure*. "It's part of being a decent human, to be tested for STDs. It's just disgusting behavior when people don't."

SCARLETT JOHANSSON

"I don't think there's any kind of preparation for sudden celebrity," Johansson (right, with Redford in *Whisperer*) has said about fame. "You're buying a slice of pizza and somebody's outside photographing you. . . . That's not normal!"

JODIE FOSTER

THEN After making her bare-bottomed debut in a Coppertone ad at 3, Foster appeared in more than 50 TV shows by age 12. Two years later she was an Academy Award nominee for her provocative role as a child prostitute in *Taxi Driver* (1976).

NOW What hasn't Jodie Foster accomplished in her 45 years? She graduated magna cum laude from Yale in 1985, snagged two Oscars before she was 30, then turned to directing and producing. Along the way she showed the next generation how to avoid the pitfalls of early celebrity. Famously tight-lipped about her private life, she refuses to identify the father of her sons Charles, 9, and Kit, 6. In April she starred with current child sensation Abigail Breslin in the adventure-comedy *Nim's Island*.

JENNIFER CONNELLY

THEN Connelly, only 14, scored the coveted role of Sarah in the Jim Henson fantasy *Labyrinth*, costarring David Bowie. **NOW** Happily married to Brit actor Paul Bettany and a mom to two boys, Connelly, 37, has a stellar résumé, including indie grit like *Requiem for a Dream*, and took home a Best Supporting Actress Oscar for 2001's *A Beautiful Mind*. Next up: *He's Just Not That into You*, costarring Drew Barrymore and Scarlett Johansson.

LEONARDO DiCAPRIO

THEN Stole scenes in TV series like *Parenthood* and *Growing Pains*; broke though as a movie star opposite Robert De Niro in *This Boy's Life*.

NOW Launched into the Hollywood stratosphere at 23 by 1997's *Titanic*; has been director Martin Scorsese's go-to guy ever since, in *Gangs of New York, The Aviator* and Best Picture Oscar winner *The Departed*. DiCaprio, 33, has received three Oscar nominations (the latest for 2006's *Blood Diamond*) and plaudits for his environmental activism. He has been dating Israeli model Bar Refaeli since 2006.

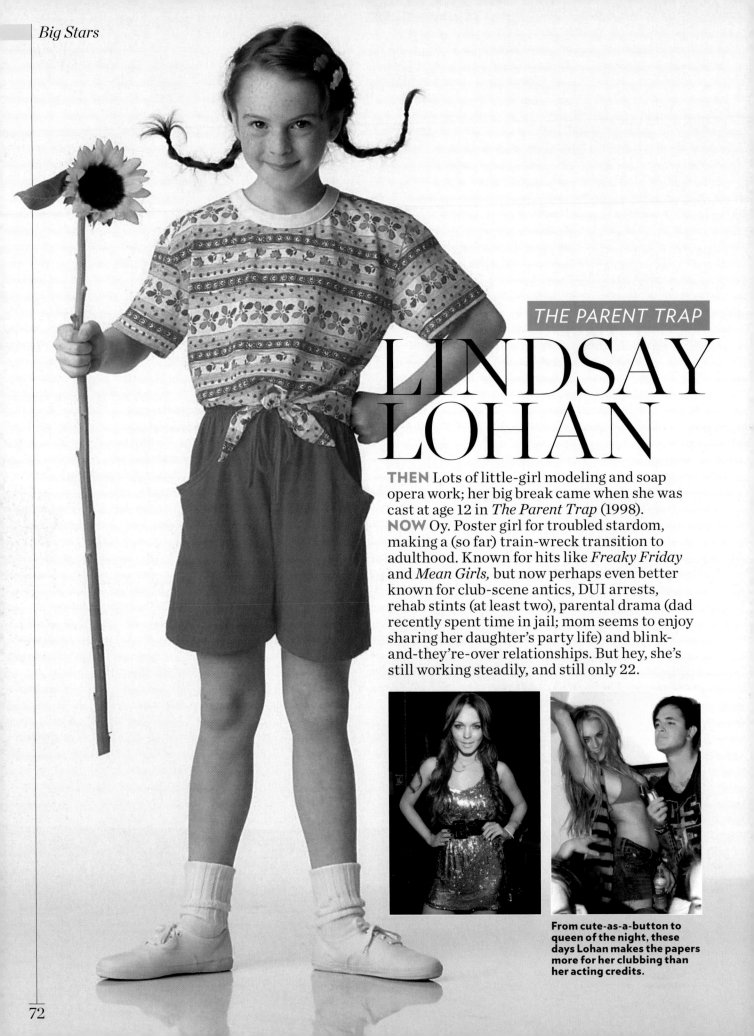

THE PARENT TRAP

LINDSAY LOHAN

THEN Lots of little-girl modeling and soap opera work; her big break came when she was cast at age 12 in *The Parent Trap* (1998). **NOW** Oy. Poster girl for troubled stardom, making a (so far) train-wreck transition to adulthood. Known for hits like *Freaky Friday* and *Mean Girls,* but now perhaps even better known for club-scene antics, DUI arrests, rehab stints (at least two), parental drama (dad recently spent time in jail; mom seems to enjoy sharing her daughter's party life) and blink-and-they're-over relationships. But hey, she's still working steadily, and still only 22.

From cute-as-a-button to queen of the night, these days Lohan makes the papers more for her clubbing than her acting credits.

"If they didn't have each other, they wouldn't be where they are now," says a source. "They are best friends."

MARY-KATE & ASHLEY OLSEN

THEN Making their TV debut at 15 months, sharing the role of Michelle Tanner on the ABC sitcom *Full House*. Next came made-for-TV movies, albums ("Brother for Sale"), dolls, clothing videos and a financial empire worth hundreds of millions.
NOW In 2004 Mary-Kate entered rehab for an eating disorder. Later that year the twins enrolled in New York University, but their college stint didn't last long. Their paths soon diverged. Today the 22-year-olds split their time between New York and Los Angeles, where they maintain separate homes. The pair are regulars on the party circuit and have been linked to a revolving cast of boyfriends. Ashley also spends time working on their clothing lines, and Mary-Kate will next be seen in an upcoming movie, *The Wackness*.

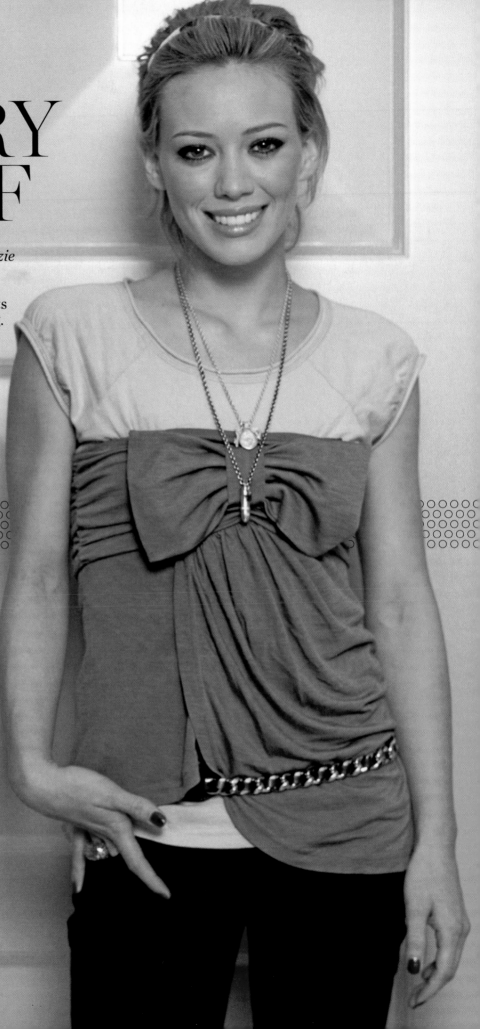

HILARY DUFF

THEN Duff was a Disney kid turned empire, with the hit TV comedy *Lizzie McGuire,* a clothing line, her own perfume and even a Barbie doll. **NOW** She's turned pop star with hits like "Come Clean" and is still acting. After film fluff like *The Perfect Man* and *Material Girls* (with sister Haylie), she starred in May's gritty satire *War, Inc.* "Nobody wanted to take a chance on me, because I'd been typecast," says Duff, 20, who's focusing on "darker, more mature" projects. "It was nice to challenge myself and do something nobody would expect me to do."

"I don't think there's a certain step-by-step guide" to avoiding the pitfalls of early fame, says Duff. "What's helped is keeping people I love around me. I don't have to do it by myself, I don't think I have all the answers."

SABRINA, THE TEENAGE WITCH
MELISSA JOAN HART

THEN A showbiz vet by junior high, Hart made hundreds of kiddie commercials—her first at age 4 for a bath toy—and appeared as a teen sage in Nickelodeon's *Clarissa Explains It All* before morphing at 19 into *Sabrina the Teenage Witch*, which ran for seven smash seasons.

NOW Despite a nearly nude 1999 photo shoot for *Maxim* magazine (cover line: "Your Favorite Witch Without a Stitch!"), Hart, 32, has been keeping things family-friendly: After Sabrina wrapped in '03, she turned her Italian nuptials to rocker Mark Wilkerson, lead singer of the band Course

of Nature, into a six-part reality show the same year. In 2007 she helped ABC Family score its highest ratings ever starring with Mario Lopez in *Holiday in Handcuffs*. But without a doubt, Hart's proudest productions have been sons Mason, 2, and Braydon, 3 months. "Between all my boys," she told PEOPLE earlier this year, "I've literally grown three hearts!"

Danes and costar A.J. Langer (see page 42) played disaffected high-schoolers in the short-lived *My So-Called Life*.

MY SO-CALLED LIFE
CLAIRE DANES

THEN Won a Golden Globe at age 15 as Angela Chase, the angsty high school sophomore on the fleeting critical success *My So-Called Life* (1994-95).

NOW Her TV show vanished after 19 episodes, but it was enough time for Danes to become one of her generation's leading actresses. Minus two years at Yale, she has worked nonstop—reciting Shakespeare with Leonardo DiCaprio in 1996's *William Shakespeare's Romeo & Juliet*, battling beside Schwarzenegger in 2003's *Terminator 3: Rise of the Machines* and bowing on Broadway as Eliza Doolittle in *Pygmalion*. Chosen one of PEOPLE's Most Beautiful at 18, Danes, 29, is dating actor Hugh Dancy and is the new face of Gucci jewelry.

THEN Popped up as a guest on TV series ranging from *Walker, Texas Ranger* to *Roseanne*, plus small parts in feature films *This Boy's Life* (in 1993, with current pal Leonardo DiCaprio) and *Deconstructing Harry* (1997).

NOW In 2002 he debuted in what has become his signature role: Peter Parker in the über-successful *Spider-Man* trilogy, but Maguire's staggering ascent began earlier, playing opposite Reese Witherspoon in 1998's *Pleasantville* and Michael Douglas in 2000's *Wonder Boys*. In 2006, Maguire, 33, and then-fiancée Jennifer Meyer, daughter of Universal Studios president Ron Meyer, welcomed a daughter, Ruby. A year later they tied the knot.

TOBEY MAGUIRE

Longtime pals Maguire and DiCaprio (below, in '90) met when they auditioned for the series *Parenthood*; **in '04 Maguire starred in** *Spider-Man 2* **(right); his current role is Dad to 1-year-old Ruby (below right).**

In the game

Fame, fortune, massive attention . . . *then* what? The first step after stardom isn't always easy. Despite the challenges, these actors stuck with their Hollywood dream

JERRY MAGUIRE

JONATHAN LIPNICKI

THEN Seriously cuddly Ray Boyd in 1996's *Jerry Maguire*.
NOW What's to do after you're a star at age 6? Now a high school junior, Lipnicki, 17, who lives in Los Angeles, practices martial arts, plays water polo and still dips his toe in the Hollywood pool. He's due to start work on a film, *For the Love of Jade*. He also raises money for a variety of causes, including juvenile diabetes.

One of Lipnicki's best-remembered *Maguire* lines? "The human head weighs 8 lbs."

RIDER STRONG

THEN Shawn Hunter, Cory Matthews' best friend.

NOW Strong, 28, graduated from Columbia University in 2004 and has said he hopes to get an M.F.A. in writing. "Writing is my passion," the published poet told PEOPLE. "Acting is my day job." That has included the 2002 horror film *Cabin Fever*, in which five college grads rent a cabin in the woods and very bad things happen. (A sequel is awaiting release.) "I don't think *Boy Meets World* ended when it ended," he says of the afterglow. "We were popular after we were canceled because the Disney Channel was running it all the time. Now people recognize me wherever I go."

DANIELLE FISHEL

THEN Fishel's guest-star role as California fantasy girl Topanga, Cory Matthews' crush, attracted so much attention that producers quickly added her to the sitcom full-time.

NOW Fishel, 27, went on to small TV and movie roles (*National Lampoon Presents Dorm Daze*) and became a spokeswoman for NutriSystem and a correspondent for *The Tyra Banks Show*. (There was also a little problem of a DWI arrest.) She looks back fondly on *Boy*: "I realized from a young age how hard it is to work regularly in this industry," she said in an interview with the UCLA student newspaper, "and I felt very blessed from the time I was young."

BEN SAVAGE

THEN The show's central character, Cory Matthews, who grew up goofily from tween to teen.

NOW After *Boy* he went off to Stanford and got a degree in political science ("my four years to just be a normal kid," he told CinemaSource.com). He recently directed one independent movie, *Car Babes*, and costarred in another, *Palo Alto*, a college coming-of-age story. Ben, 27, is still single, still actor Fred Savage's little brother and believes he and his *Boy* castmates were blessed by the show's steady, low-key success: "We were just good, stable kids."

WILL FRIEDLE

THEN Cory's brother Eric

NOW After *Boy* ended in 2000, "I did a bunch of failed shows," Friedle, 31, told PEOPLE. (There was also a film, *National Lampoon's Gold Diggers*.) Friedle found a steady gig for two years providing the voice of Ron Stoppable on the Disney animated series *Kim Possible*, which ended in 2007. He says the most shocking thing about his *Boy* years was how normal they were. "Our *E! True Hollywood Story* would be the most boring thing on television since the opening of Al Capone's vault," says Friedle. "The E! voice-over guy would be like, 'And they all got along.'"

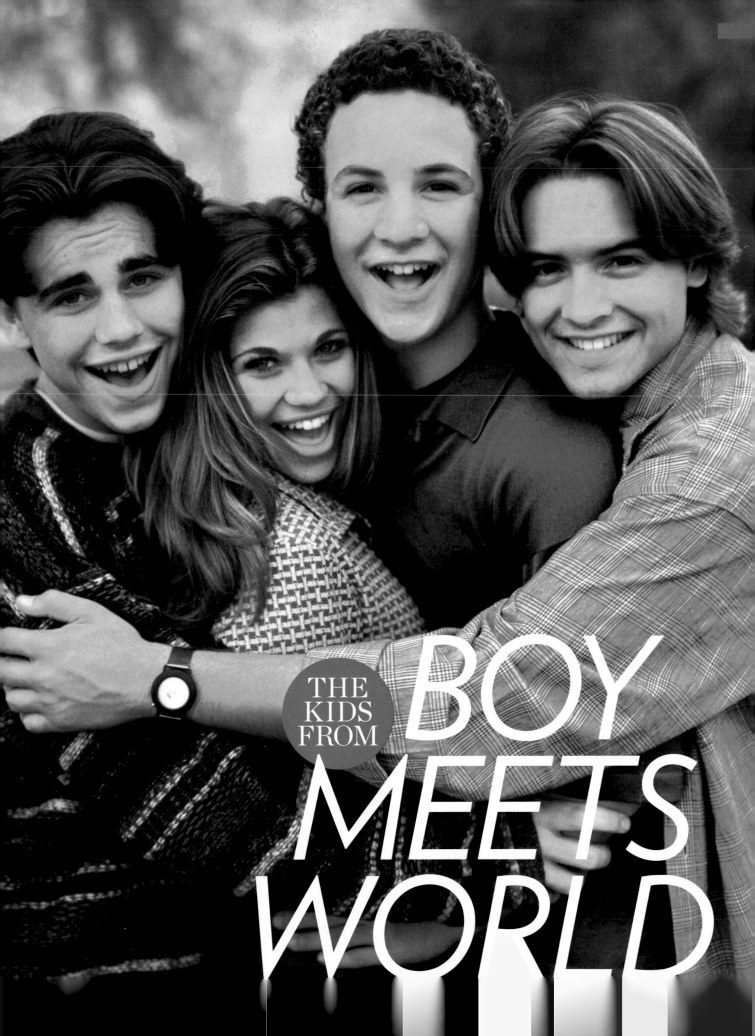

THE KIDS FROM BOY MEETS WORLD

DAVID FAUSTINO

THEN Budrick "Bud" Bundy on the hit FOX sitcom *Married . . . with Children* from 1986 to 1997. **NOW** Faustino's first role came at 3 months, playing a baby on a Lily Tomlin special. These days the actor, 34 and divorced with no children, continues his career working on small-budget films and television series, including *RoboDoc,* starring Alan Thicke, and *Working Title,* costarring Ed Asner.

Chlumsky starred alongside Macaulay Culkin in *My Girl* but went on without him in the sequel.

MY GIRL

ANNA CHLUMSKY

THEN Vada Stultenfuss, a little girl dealing with big issues in 1991's *My Girl*. Gives Macaulay Culkin his first screen kiss.

NOW A few years later, Chlumsky stepped away from it all, eventually earning a degree in international studies from the University of Chicago. An aspiring food writer—her father, Frank, is a chef—she later moved to New York to work as a researcher for the Zagat's restaurant guide and hunt acting jobs. Chlumsky, 27, has had small stage and movie roles and, notably, appeared as Tina Fey's romantic rival, Liz Lemler, in a 2007 episode of *30 Rock*. In Oct. 2007 she announced her engagement to Shaun So, 26, an army reservist who had served in Afghanistan. They married in March 2008.

THE COSBY SHOW

TEMPESTT BLEDSOE

THEN Vanessa, the smart-aleck, sometimes whiny middle child.

NOW In 2008 Bledsoe starred alongside Erik Estrada in the Oxygen network's movie of the week *Husband for Hire*. A graduate of NYU with a degree in finance, Bledsoe, 34, has also been a contestant on the reality shows *Celebrity Fit Club* and *Fear Factor*. She is the voice of Riley on Disney's animated *The Replacements*.

MALCOLM-JAMAL WARNER

THEN Theo, the likable if sometimes underachieving Huxtable.

NOW Singing, playing bass and directing; fronts his own jazz-funk group, Miles Long Band, and performed *Love & Other Social Issues*, a one-man show he wrote. Warner, 37, has directed episodes of *Malcolm & Eddie* and *Sesame Street* and appeared with Matthew McConaughey in *Fool's Gold*.

LISA BONET
a.k.a. LILAKOI MOON

THEN Denise, the funky Huxtable.

NOW Still funky. A mom of two (Zoe, 19, with ex Lenny Kravitz; and Lola, 11 months, with boyfriend Jason Momoa of *Stargate Atlantis*), the actress, 40, changed her name to Lilakoi Moon in the '90s and avoids Hollywood—though she will appear in the Coen brothers' next film, *Gambit*, alongside Jennifer Aniston and Sir Ben Kingsley.

KESHIA KNIGHT PULLIAM

THEN Little Rudy, the adorable one.

NOW A Spelman College grad, Pulliam, 29, has a recurring role on the TBS sitcom *Tyler Perry's House of Payne*. In an effort to shed her "little girl" image, she posed for a swimsuit spread in *Black Men* mag in '04 and vamped in a Chingy rap video. "As you approach 30," she says, "it's this feeling of, 'I'm, like, for real an adult.'"

RAVEN-SYMONÉ

THEN Olivia, Denise's cute-as-a-button stepdaughter, beginning in 1989.

NOW A 22-year-old gazillionaire, thanks to her Disney Channel TV hits *That's So Raven* and *The Cheetah Girls* and a successful recording career. The actress—born Raven-Simoné Christina Pearman—starred alongside Martin Lawrence in the 2008 film *College Road Trip*.

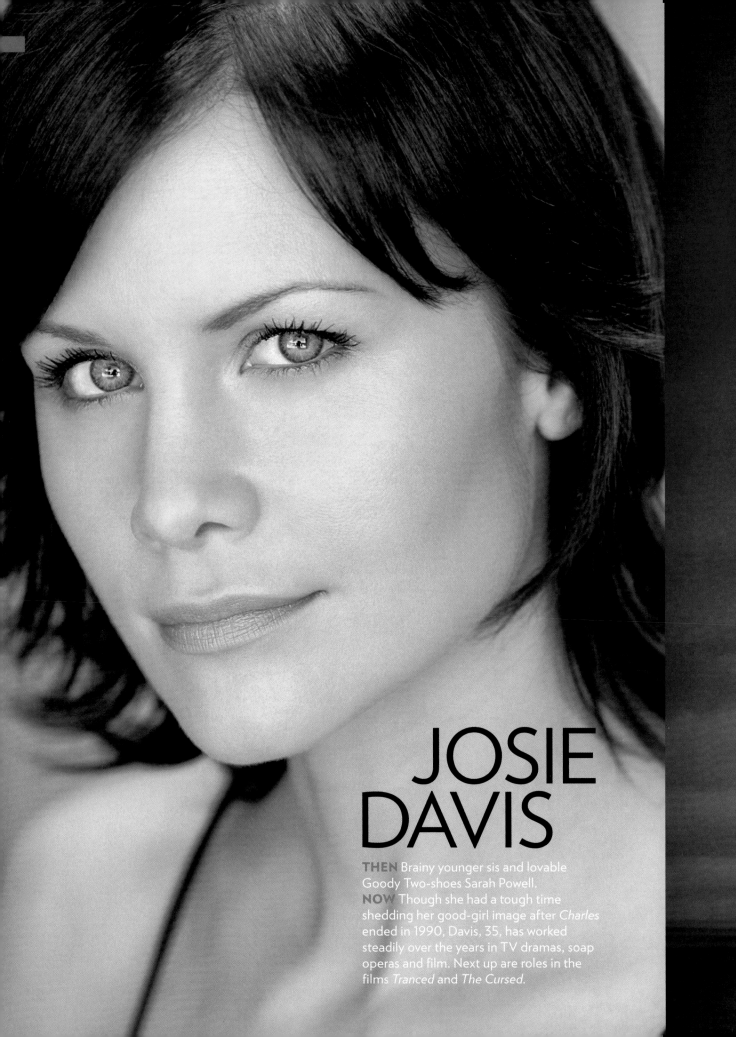

JOSIE DAVIS

THEN Brainy younger sis and lovable Goody Two-shoes Sarah Powell.
NOW Though she had a tough time shedding her good-girl image after *Charles* ended in 1990, Davis, 35, has worked steadily over the years in TV dramas, soap operas and film. Next up are roles in the films *Tranced* and *The Cursed*.

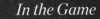

Davis (left) and Eggert flank co-star Scott Baio in *Charles'* second TV incarnation.

CHARLES IN CHARGE

NICOLE EGGERT

THEN Eggert came to public notice playing teenage Jamie Powell in the syndicated version of the sitcom *Charles in Charge*, which starred Scott Baio.

NOW From there, she swam on to play *Baywatch* lifeguard Summer Quinn. Her most recent film is 2008's *Loaded*. Now 36, she is married and has a daughter, Dilyn, 10. Fun fact: Eggert appeared on the cover of Sugar Ray's debut album, *Lemonade and Brownies*.

LARK VOORHIES

THEN Lisa Turtle, the fashion-obsessed, unwilling object of Screech's affection.

NOW Voorhies, 34, has turned her attention to developing her own projects. The budding writer is actively involved with the Writers Guild of America and recently completed her first full-length screenplay, *The Hope for Pandora's Box*. Voorhies can be seen in the upcoming film *The Next Hit*.

THE KIDS FROM
SAVED BY THE BELL

TIFFANI THIESSEN

THEN All American girl-next-door Kelly Kapowski.

NOW After *Saved by the Bell*, Thiessen, 34, tackled more television, most notably as *90210*'s villainous Valerie Malone. In 2005 she started a production company, Tit 4 Tat Productions, and directed a well-received short film, *Just Pray*. Thiessen says she hopes her next project is motherhood.

ELIZABETH BERKLEY

THEN Brainy A-student Jessie Spano.

NOW Although famously bashed by critics for 1995's *Showgirls*, the actress has worked steadily in both films and TV and currently hosts the Bravo reality show *Step It Up and Dance*. Berkley, 35, who is married to Greg Lauren, nephew of designer Ralph, also runs www.ask-elizabeth.com, a Web site that helps young women with self-esteem problems.

MARIO LOPEZ

THEN Lovable, muscle-bound jock A.C. Slater.

NOW Lopez, 30, has been acting regularly on television since saying goodbye to Slater (and the curly mullet) in '94. Thanks to a second-place finish on the third season of *Dancing with the Stars,* his own star has been on the rise: The Latin hunk has worked as a correspondent for *Extra,* hosted the Miss Universe, Miss America and Miss Teen USA pageants and appeared on Broadway in *A Chorus Line*.

DUSTIN DIAMOND

THEN Bayside High's resident squeaky-voiced geek, Samuel "Screech" Powers.

NOW Despite a couple of setbacks (financial trouble and the release of a sex tape in '06), the actor and stand-up comedian has elevated his profile with decidedly un-Screech-like stints on VH1's *Celebrity Fit Club*. Diamond, 31, lives in Wisconsin with his girlfriend, Jennifer, and will release a comedy album, *Comedy Ain't Pretty,* this year.

MARK-PAUL GOSSELAAR

THEN Lovable pretty boy Zack Morris.

NOW Working and riding his bikes. Appeared in the 1998 movie *Dead Man on Campus* and the TV series *NYPD Blue, Commander in Chief* (with actress Geena Davis) and HBO's *John from Cincinnati*. Met his wife, Lisa Ann Russell, 37, when she guest-starred on *Saved;* they have two children. An avid track cyclist, Gosselaar, 34, will next appear in TNT's legal series *Raising the Bar*.

JALEEL WHITE

THEN *Family Matters* übernerd Steve Urkel (1989-1998).
NOW Thanks largely to White's Urkel, *Family Matters* ran for more than 200 episodes, and at one point he even had a cereal named after him (Urkel-o's). When it ended, White, now 31, earned a B.A. from UCLA's film school and has spent much of the time since working on scripts and hoping to create a hit. He had a small part in *Dreamgirls,* appeared in a 2007 episode of *Boston Legal* and was the voice of Sonic the Hedgehog in the cartoon series.

ANDRE
TINA MAJORINO

THEN Toni, the little girl who befriends a harbor seal in 1994's *Andre*.
NOW Played computer ace Mac on the series *Veronica Mars,* costarred opposite Jon Heder in *Napoleon Dynamite* and has a recurring role, as Heather Tuttle, in HBO's *Big Love*. Curious fact: Majorino, 23, is a black belt in the martial art of Tang Soo Do.

She made "Tomorrow" famous yesterday: Quinn, all dressed up in curly locks in *Annie*, and today (right).

ANNIE
AILEEN QUINN

THEN At 10, song-and-danced her way into Daddy Warbucks' and America's hearts in *Annie* (1982).
NOW After years of success in theater, most recently in the national tour of *Saturday Night Fever,* Quinn, 37, is recording her first album, the music of which she describes as "relationship driven." The still spunky redhead can also be seen in an upcoming indie film, *Multiple Sarcasms.*

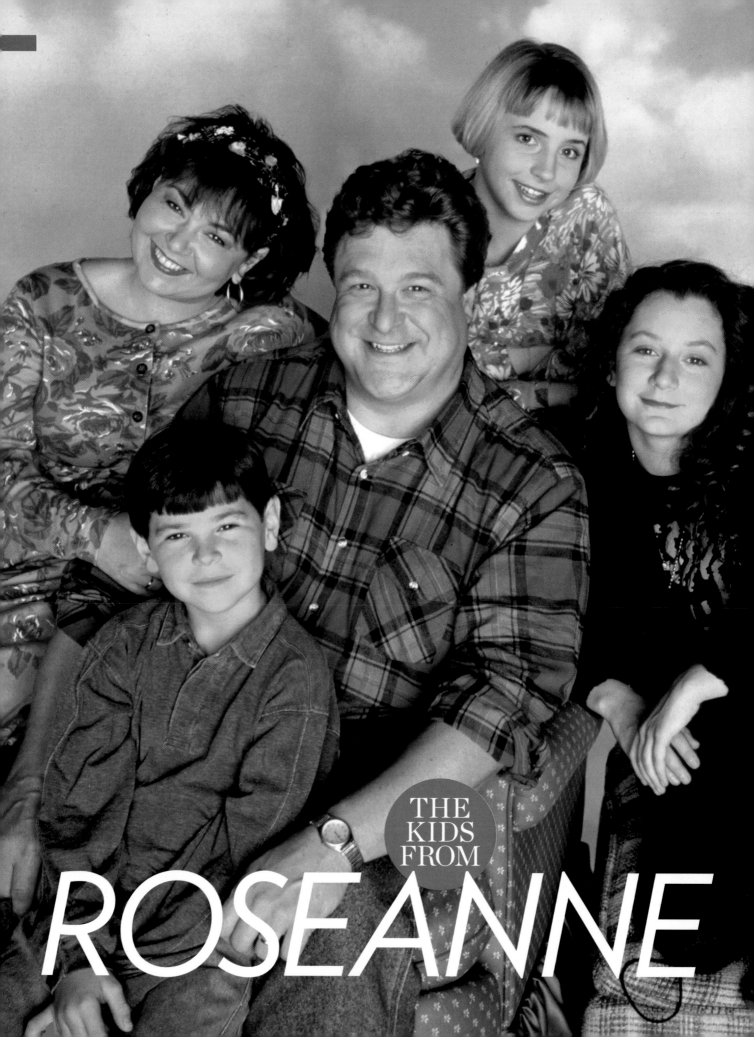

THE
KIDS
FROM

ROSEANNE

ALICIA GORANSON

THEN Boy-crazy Becky.

NOW An on-again-off-again presence on *Roseanne* as she juggled her career and a Vassar course load, the single Goranson, 33, has done TV only sparingly since her Becky days (when she was known as Lecy Goranson). Screen credits include *Boys Don't Cry* and *Love, Ludlow.* "I much prefer theater and film, in that order," she told curvemag.com. Still, it's hard to deny the cache of having appeared (as the birth mother of a child the character Charlotte plans to adopt) in the final episode of *Sex and the City.* She also appeared in *Law & Order: Special Victims Unit.*

SARA GILBERT

THEN Disaffected, wisecracking Darlene.

NOW A succession of TV roles (*24*, *ER* and *Twins*) has made Gilbert, 33, a familiar face in the prime-time firmament. In 2004 she revealed that she is gay and that her partner, TV writer-producer Allison Adler, had recently delivered a baby boy, Levi Hank. Three years later Gilbert gave birth to the couple's second child, a daughter, Sawyer. Recently Gilbert has appeared on the CBS sitcom *The Big Bang Theory* opposite Johnny Galecki—who portrayed her onscreen boyfriend and husband, David Healy, in *Roseanne.*

MICHAEL FISHMAN

THEN D.J., the little brother.

NOW Left showbiz at age 18 to be a husband and father. Now that his son, 8, and daughter, 5, are getting older, Fishman, 26, is venturing back into acting. "My priorities have always been focused on what I think are the right directions," he says. "I want to work, but I make time to do things with the kids, because I only get one shot at that." As for his nine years on *Roseanne,* Fishman has only positive memories. He remains close with the cast and crew and says his children "see Roseanne as an extra grandma they go and see from time to time."

HALLIE KATE EISENBERG

THEN The kid from those memorable '90s Pepsi commercials (and, later, the 1998 film *Paulie*).

NOW Fifteen years old and a vegetarian who juggles and also enjoys competing as an equestrienne, she appeared in the 2006 film *How to Eat Fried Worms.* Eisenberg told an online interviewer in 2006 that she hopes to become a doctor. She was featured in the independent film *P.J.* Her older brother Jesse received good notices in *The Squid and the Whale.*

Though she gained fame in a Pepsi commercial, Eisenberg no longer drinks much soda.

STACY KEANAN

THEN At 12, Keanan played the coveted kid on *My Two Dads,* then graduated to a self-absorbed teen on *Step by Step.*

NOW After studying art history at UCLA, Keanan, 33, has returned to acting in indie flicks like 2006's *Hidden Secrets* and the upcoming Amish comedy *Holyman Undercover.* Her recent run in a production of *Moment in the Sun* was "a death-defying experience," she says.

Keanan acted with dads Paul Reiser and Greg Evigan.

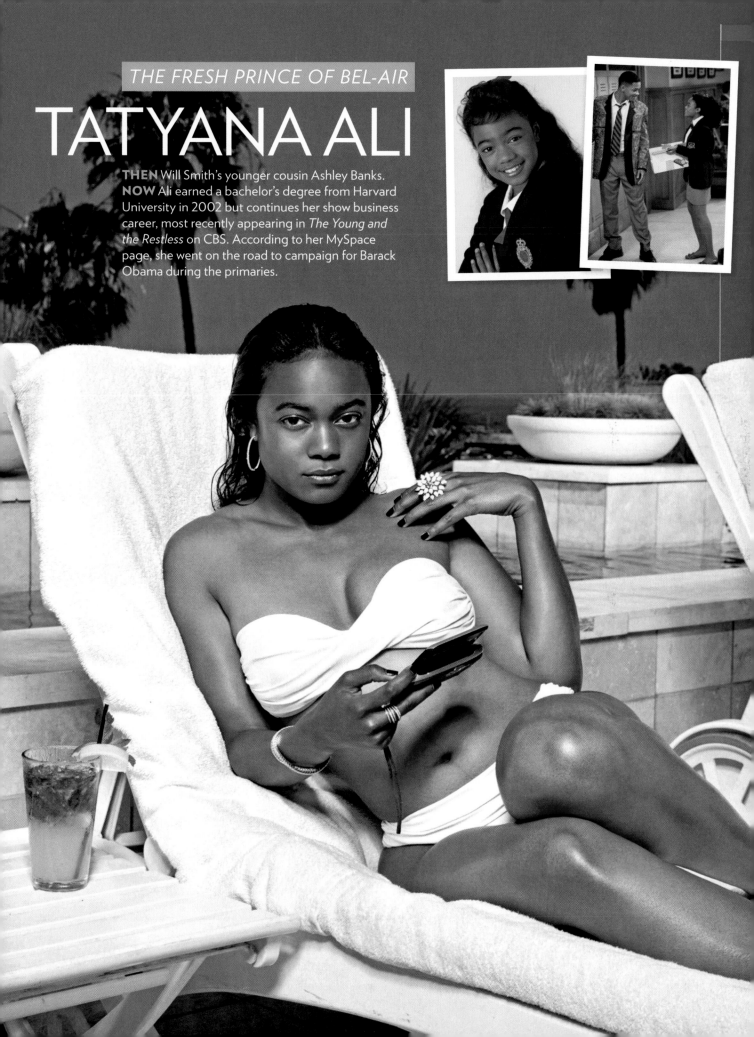

THE FRESH PRINCE OF BEL-AIR

TATYANA ALI

THEN Will Smith's younger cousin Ashley Banks.
NOW Ali earned a bachelor's degree from Harvard University in 2002 but continues her show business career, most recently appearing in *The Young and the Restless* on CBS. According to her MySpace page, she went on the road to campaign for Barack Obama during the primaries.

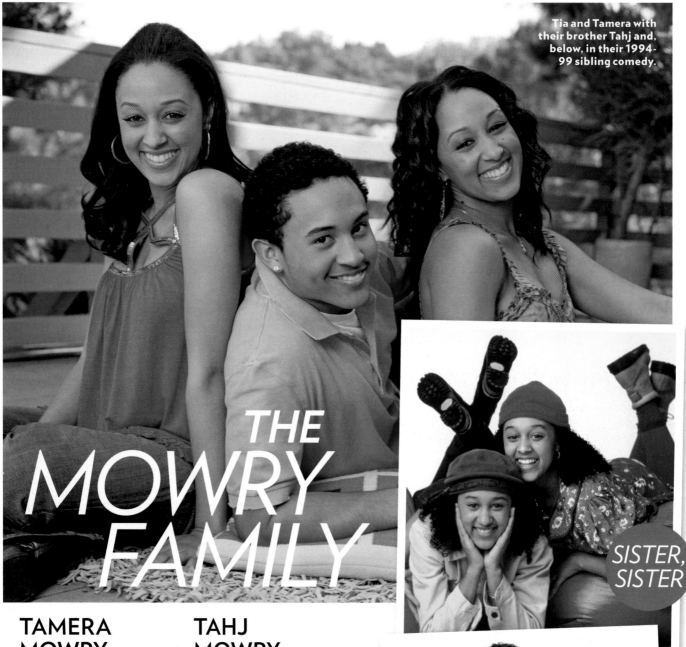

Tia and Tamera with their brother Tahj and, below, in their 1994-99 sibling comedy.

THE MOWRY FAMILY

SISTER, SISTER

SMART GUY

TAMERA MOWRY

THEN She played Tamera Campbell, the boy-crazy half of the twin team on *Sister, Sister*.

NOW After nabbing her psych degree from Pepperdine, Mowry, 29, graduated to more grown-up fare playing Dr. Kayla Thornton on the Lifetime drama *Strong Medicine*. Mowry next coproduces and stars with twin Tia in the Lifetime romantic comedy *Double Date*. "It's always a blast working with Tia, because we never feel it's actually work," says Mowry. "We have this natural chemistry, maybe because we're such opposites. Now that we are older, we can accept, own and learn from our different personalities."

TAHJ MOWRY

THEN He guest-starred on *Full House* and *Sister, Sister* before landing his own sitcom, *Smart Guy*.

NOW Focused on football at Georgia's Savannah State University and the University of Wyoming, where he played running back. Last year Mowry transferred to his sisters' alma mater, Pepperdine University, where he's studying merchandising. He has also returned to acting, landing guest gigs on sister Tia's show *The Game* and *Desperate Housewives*, as well as a lead role in the 2007 Ice Cube comedy *Are We Done Yet?*. Next up is teen horror flick *Bad Meat* and a record deal.

TIA MOWRY HARDRICT

THEN *Sister, Sister*'s feistier twin.
NOW Younger than her sister by two minutes, Tia, 29, studied psychology alongside sister Tamera at Pepperdine University before heading back to TV on the CW hit *The Game*. "It's really let me stretch and prove I'm no longer a little girl," says Tia. In April she wed Cory Hardrict, who acted with the twins in January's *Hollywood Horror*. Despite marriage and somewhat diverging career paths, she's still superclose to her sister. In fact, "Tamera's going to be filming her new show [*Roommates*] on the same lot as *The Game*," says Tia gleefully. "So we can have lunch together!"

KEISHA CASTLE-HUGHES

THEN At 13, she became the youngest actress ever to score a Best Actress Oscar nod for her turn in 2002's *Whale Rider.*

NOW Castle-Hughes has continued to work, as the Queen of Naboo in *Star Wars: Episode III—Revenge of the Sith* and as Mary in *The Nativity Story.* Her most surprising role, though, has been motherhood: In 2007, at 17, Castle-Hughes gave birth to daughter Felicity-Amore; the father is Bradley Hull, 20, her boyfriend of five years. She plans to continue working. "Just because I have a baby, it doesn't mean that my career is going to go kaput," she said last year. "I have a really ambitious streak in me. I want to do it now more than I ever did."

"It hurt," Castle-Hughes has said about some media outlets' reaction to her pregnancy: "I was supposed to be able to go, 'Wow, I'm having a baby and this is amazing.'"

MOLLY RINGWALD

THEN Ringwald was already a showbiz vet, with appearances on *The New Mickey Mouse Club, Diff'rent Strokes* and *The Facts of Life,* before landing her breakthrough role, at 16, in the 1984 Gen X classic *Sixteen Candles.* The following year *The Breakfast Club* solidified her screen image as a brainy—if a tad insecure—beauty.

NOW Ringwald, 40, spoofed her teen roles in the 2001 film *Not Another Teen Movie.* In '03 she gave birth to daughter Mathilda Ereni with second husband Panio Gianopoulos, an editor and writer she married in '07. Ringwald has appeared on Broadway in a variety of plays, including *Cabaret* and *Enchanted April.* She can be seen this summer on ABC Family's *The Secret Life of the American Teenager.*

Ringwald, the muse of writer-director John Hughes, starred in a trilogy of teenage angst films, including 1985's *The Breakfast Club.*

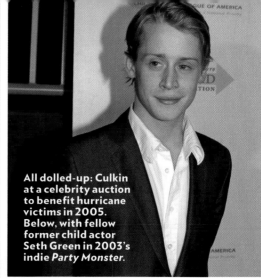

All dolled-up: Culkin at a celebrity auction to benefit hurricane victims in 2005. Below, with fellow former child actor Seth Green in 2003's indie *Party Monster*.

MACAULAY CULKIN

THEN Arguably the most successful and recognizable child star of the '90s, Culkin, at 10, busted two bonehead burglars—and box office records—as Kevin McCallister in the 1990 classic *Home Alone*.

NOW Culkin, 27, has flown under the radar for the past few years, appearing in independent, artsy projects and writing a semiautobiographical book, *Junior,* in 2006. His path hasn't always been smooth: He left the profession at 14, sued his parents for control over his own finances (and won) and divorced at 20 after two years of marriage. "I don't know what people want from me," he told TIME magazine. In 2005 Culkin received unwanted attention for his friendship with Michael Jackson when he testified against "ridiculous" allegations Jackson had molested him as a child. One positive presence in his life today is his girlfriend of six years, Mila Kunis (*That '70s Show; Forgetting Sarah Marshall*). Though the couple are reluctant to discuss their relationship, Kunis recently told *Parade* magazine that Culkin's unconventional upbringing "made him who he is" and called him "an incredible human being."

Show me the monkey: Birch starred with a light-fingered simian before moving on to more grown-up fare.

THORA BIRCH

THEN At 12, tried to tame a pickpocketing pet in *Monkey Trouble* (1994).
NOW After launching into the critical mainstream as disillusioned teen Jane Burnham in 1999's Best Picture winner *American Beauty*, Birch, 26, continues to have success in small, art-house projects (including 2001's cult hit *Ghost World*).

Martin (with husband Keith and daughter Margaret Heather) starred with Chris Burke (below) in *Life Goes On*.

LIFE GOES ON
KELLIE MARTIN

THEN The Thatchers' smart, socially awkward daughter Becca. **NOW** After *Life*, earned an art history degree from Yale. Professionally, Martin, 32, spent two seasons on *ER* and has starred in 10 *Mystery Woman* movies for the Hallmark Channel. In 1999 she married lawyer Keith Christian; in 2006 they had a daughter, Margaret Heather, whose middle name honored Martin's sister, who died of lupus at 19.

FIELD OF DREAMS

GABY HOFFMANN

THEN Played Kevin Costner's daughter in *Field of Dreams.* "I spent all day playing baseball and flirting with Ray Liotta," she recalls. "I loved it."
NOW Raised in New York City's historic Chelsea Hotel, with acting in her DNA—her single-name mom, Viva, starred in Andy Warhol movies—Hoffmann, 26, took a five-year break from acting to attend Bard College. She studied literature, art history, political science—"pretty much everything that caught my fancy," she says. Now, she's tip-toeing her way back into the biz. "I was going to be a million things, but not an actress," she says. "I was in denial a long time before I thought, 'This is what I really [love] to do.'"

Hoffmann, above, and with Costner, left, in *Dreams.* "[Being a famous] child is something you never get away from, it does something to you," she says. "It took a long time to sort through that."

Crossing over: Osment in 2007 and, inset, in his breakout role as the boy who could commune with the dead.

THE SIXTH SENSE

HALEY JOEL OSMENT

THEN He saw dead people in—and got an Oscar nomination for—1999's *The Sixth Sense.*
NOW Osment, who first appeared in *Forrest Gump* and who made *Sense* when he was 10, later starred in *Pay It Forward* and Steven Spielberg's *A.I.: Artificial Intelligence.* Like many child stars, he also hit a bump in the road: In July 2006, Osment, then 18, flipped his 1995 Saturn and smashed into a mailbox. When he was hospitalized, his blood alcohol was found to be double the legal limit. Osment pleaded no contest to misdemeanor drunken driving. A Canadian newspaper ran the headline, "He Sees Dead People, Not Mailboxes." Now his younger sister Emily (*Hannah Montana*) is following in his acting footsteps.

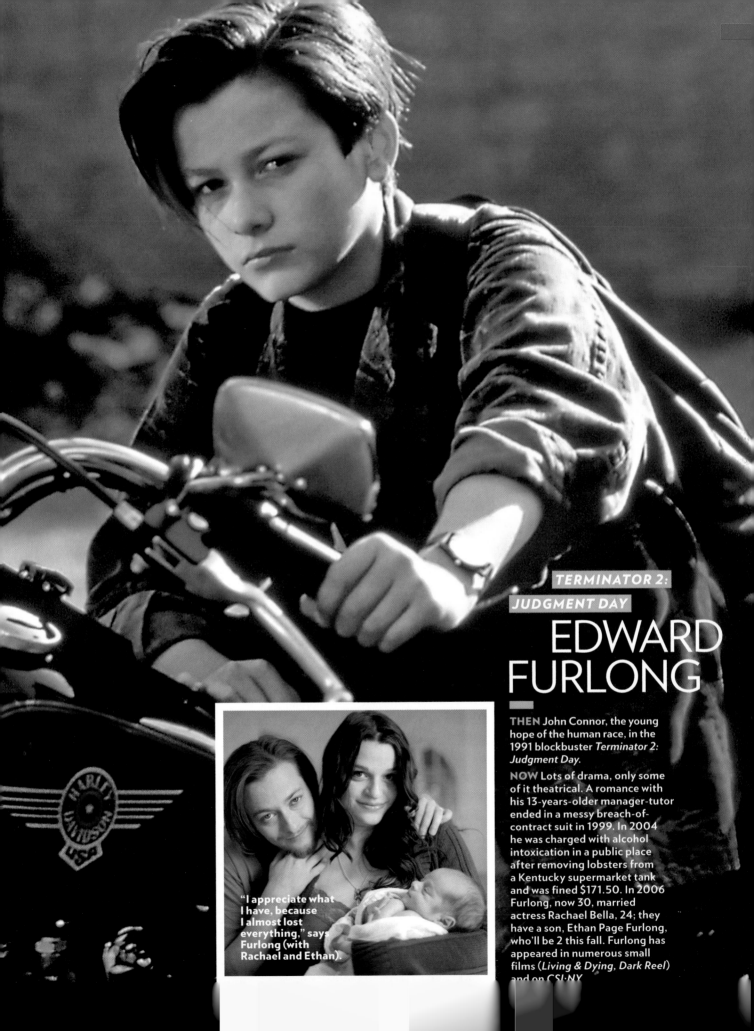

TERMINATOR 2: JUDGMENT DAY

EDWARD FURLONG

THEN John Connor, the young hope of the human race, in the 1991 blockbuster *Terminator 2: Judgment Day*.

NOW Lots of drama, only some of it theatrical. A romance with his 13-years-older manager-tutor ended in a messy breach-of-contract suit in 1999. In 2004 he was charged with alcohol intoxication in a public place after removing lobsters from a Kentucky supermarket tank and was fined $171.50. In 2006 Furlong, now 30, married actress Rachael Bella, 24; they have a son, Ethan Page Furlong, who'll be 2 this fall. Furlong has appeared in numerous small films (*Living & Dying, Dark Reel*) and on *CSI·NY*.

"I appreciate what I have, because I almost lost everything," says Furlong (with Rachael and Ethan).

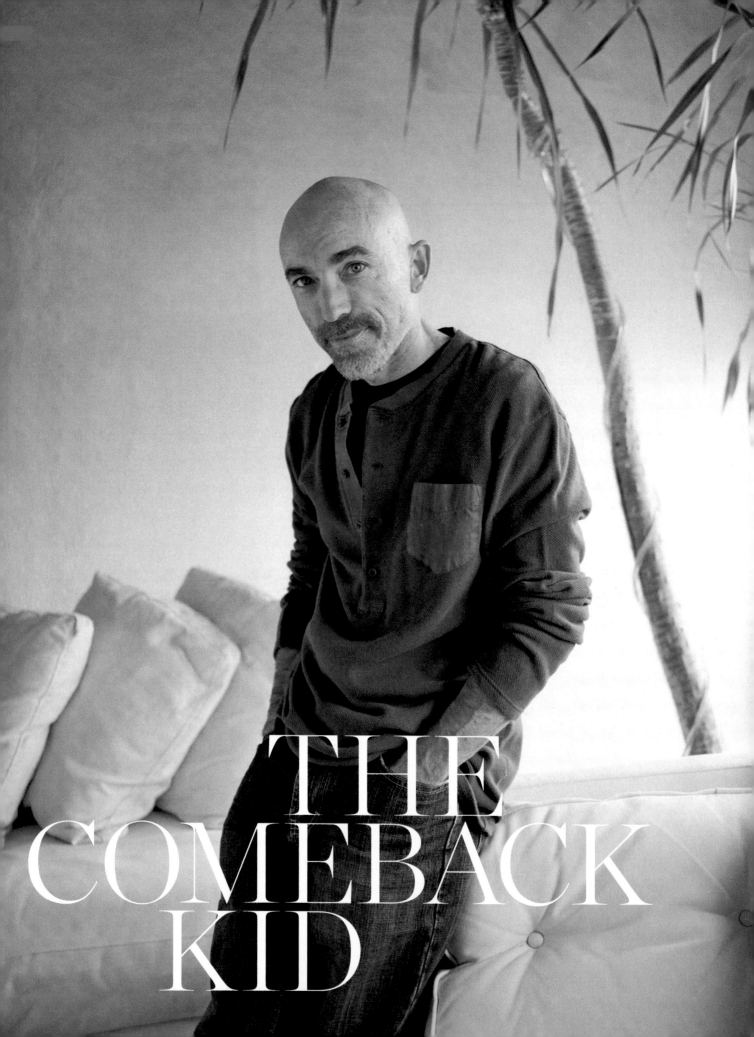

THE COMEBACK KID

Haley, second from left, in 1979's *Breaking Away*; below, in *Bears*.

THE BAD NEWS BEARS

JACKIE EARLE HALEY

THEN Too cool teen Kelly Leak in the original *Bad News Bears*, Haley's Harley-riding, home-run-slugging naughty boy sent him on the fast track to superstar status until Hollywood's harsh standards and puberty caught up with him.

NOW Thanks to notable performances in 2006's *All the King's Men* and *Little Children,* the latter receiving a Best Supporting Actor Oscar nod, Haley is a star rediscovered. In the years following the decline of his teen-idol status, Haley says he struggled to find an identity that wasn't wrapped up in his earlier celebrity. To make ends meet, he delivered pizza, drove limos and worked as a security guard. He eventually left Hollywood for San Antonio, where he moved behind the camera, making commercials, and started a successful production company. It was at that point when *King's* director, Steven Zaillian, called him out of the blue and requested a meeting. Now with a full docket of films lined up, including *Winged Creatures, Watchmen* and Martin Scorsese's *Shutter Island,* Haley is humbly basking in the glow of his renewed star status. Particularly the support he's received from his Hollywood peers. "The sentiment is overwhelming," says Haley. "If I had to do it all over, I would do it all over [in the same way]."

HAPPY FEET

ELIJAH WOOD

THEN Broke into the biz at 8 with small roles in a Paula Abdul music video and *Back to the Future II* (see page 66).

NOW Wood, 27, is best known for his portrayal of complex live-action characters, most notably Frodo Baggins in the *Lord of the Rings* trilogy. But in 2006 he tackled a character of the feathery sort, the voice of Mumble the tap-dancing penguin in the family-friendly animated film *Happy Feet*. Backed by an all-star cast of Robin Williams, Nicole Kidman and Hugh Jackman, Wood and co.'s efforts helped *Feet* nab the Academy Award for Best Animated Feature Film.

STAND BY ME

WIL WHEATON

THEN Gordie Lachance in the coming-of-age classic *Stand by Me* and teen crewman Wesley Crusher on *Star Trek: The Next Generation*.

NOW A writer, voice actor and dad. Wheaton has published three books (*Just a Geek*, *Happiest Days of Our Lives* and *Dancing Barefoot*, all nonfiction) and is working on a collection of sci-fi short stories. As a voice actor, he has taken on quirky characters: Aqualad on *Teen Titans*, Cosmic Boy on *Legion of Super Heroes*. The work takes serious acting chops, he says: "You can't just be good-looking like on-camera." Happily married to wife Anne since 1999, the 35-year-old says he is enjoying another big role: dad. "My boys are teenagers now," he says of stepsons Ryan, 18, and Nolan, 16. "They're at that point in their lives where they are figuring out who they are and who they're going to be." Father-son bonding activities include playing the video game Rock Band and watching TV's *Battlestar Galactica*.

Left to right below: Wheaton today; as Wesley Crusher on *Star Trek: The Next Generation*; and with River Phoenix in *Stand by Me*.

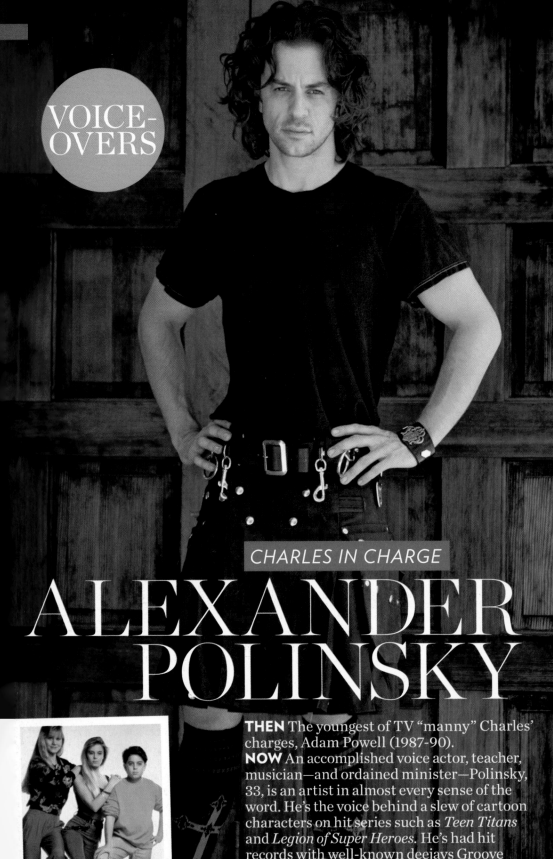

CHARLES IN CHARGE

ALEXANDER POLINSKY

Matter-Eater Lad

Control Freak

Dennis in *The Life and Times of Juniper Lee*

Headmaster on *Transformers: Animated*

THEN The youngest of TV "manny" Charles' charges, Adam Powell (1987-90).

NOW An accomplished voice actor, teacher, musician—and ordained minister—Polinsky, 33, is an artist in almost every sense of the word. He's the voice behind a slew of cartoon characters on hit series such as *Teen Titans* and *Legion of Super Heroes*. He's had hit records with well-known deejays Groove Junkies. He teaches voice acting to classes of 30 to 50 people. In his spare time, Polinsky and his equally artsy wife, Regan (a film-score composer and harpist), officiate and perform at weddings. "I don't think you can separate your art from your life," he says. "So I built art around my life, and it's been extremely fruitful these last few years."

Polinsky, celebrating his Scottish roots in a kilt he wore to the '07 Burning Man festival. "I like pants," he says, "but the freedom of a non-bifurcated garment is wonderfully refreshing."

BOY MEETS WORLD
WILL FRIEDLE

THEN Zany older brother Eric on the ABC T.G.I.F. hit.

NOW After *Boy* ended in 2000, Friedle did the quickly canceled TV series *The Random Years*, plus the box office bomb *National Lampoon's Gold Diggers*. But he scored big *off-camera* as the voice of Ron Stoppable on Disney's superhero series *Kim Possible*. He's also voiced the animated series *Batman Beyond* and *Justice League*, as well as 2005's *Chicken Little*. "You don't have to get dressed up, you don't have to wear makeup," says Friedle, 31, of the work. "You make strange facial expressions to hit the high notes or contort your body in a certain way to hit a low note. It's a different kind of letting it all hang out."

Chabert, above left, in *Party*, has lent her voice to many animated features, including, above right, *Thornberrys*.

PARTY OF FIVE
LACEY CHABERT

THEN Headstrong and precocious little sis Claudia Salinger on the long-running family drama *Party of Five*.

NOW While she still appears in front of the camera—her most memorable post-*Party* gig was the popular high school flick *Mean Girls*—Chabert also has a successful career behind the camera, lending her voice to a slew of recognizable animated characters. Her colorful credits include Meg Griffin on the first season of *Family Guy*, the inquisitive animal lover Eliza Thornberry on Nickelodeon's *The Wild Thornberrys*, *The Wild Thornberrys Movie* and *Rugrats Go Wild* and Peter Parker's love interest Gwen Stacy in *The Spectacular Spider-Man*. The busy 25-year-old is slated to appear onscreen in the upcoming films *Sherman's Way*, *In My Sleep* and *Ghosts of Girlfriends Past*.

In the Biz

After their big child-star moments, when the applause died down, they smiled, bowed politely . . . and stepped *behind* the camera (or into an executive suite) to try showbiz from another angle

→
SEE PETER TODAY!

Peter Billingsley starred as Ralphie in the holiday classic *A Christmas Story*. He went on to become a movie and TV producer.

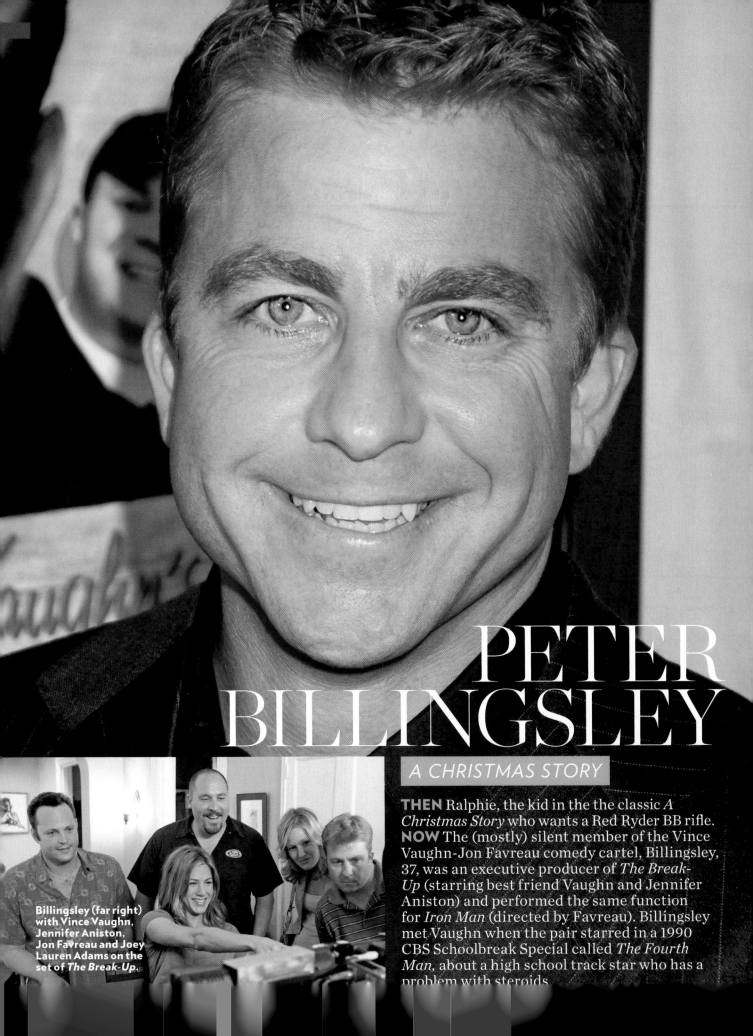

PETER BILLINGSLEY

A CHRISTMAS STORY

THEN Ralphie, the kid in the the classic *A Christmas Story* who wants a Red Ryder BB rifle.
NOW The (mostly) silent member of the Vince Vaughn-Jon Favreau comedy cartel, Billingsley, 37, was an executive producer of *The Break-Up* (starring best friend Vaughn and Jennifer Aniston) and performed the same function for *Iron Man* (directed by Favreau). Billingsley met Vaughn when the pair starred in a 1990 CBS Schoolbreak Special called *The Fourth Man,* about a high school track star who has a problem with steroids.

Billingsley (far right) with Vince Vaughn, Jennifer Aniston, Jon Favreau and Joey Lauren Adams on the set of *The Break-Up*.

"I actually got into acting to make money to go to art school," says Beckham, who dreamed of being an artist as a child.

MR. BELVEDERE
BRICE BECKHAM

THEN Bratty Wesley Owens on *Mr. Belvedere*.
NOW His production company, Drama 3/4, created the VH1 comedy *I Hate My 30s*. "It's been a long, bumpy road," says Beckham, 32, who also starred in *30s*. "But it's worth it to do our own thing."

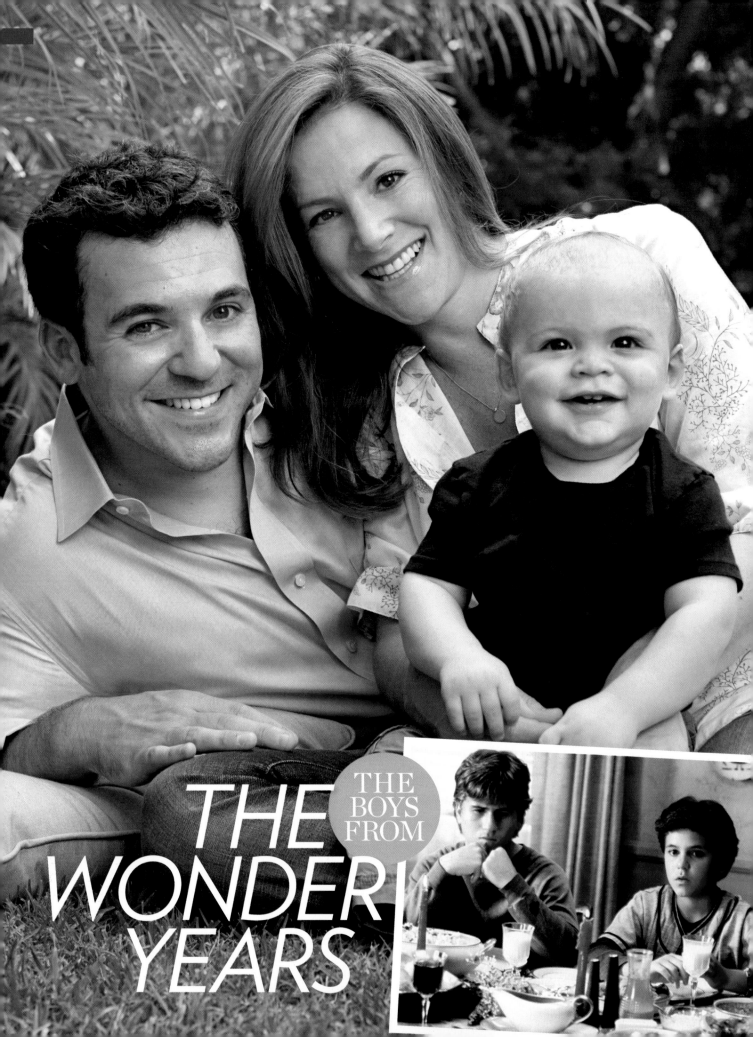

THE BOYS FROM

THE
WONDER
YEARS

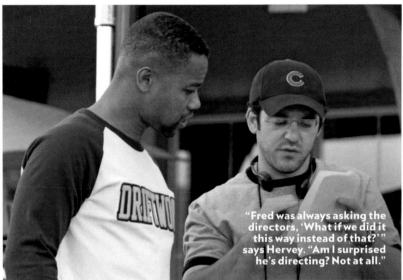

"Fred was always asking the directors, 'What if we did it this way instead of that?'" says Hervey. "Am I surprised he's directing? Not at all."

"Back home, she was the celebrity, not me," says Savage of his childhood-pal-turned-wife, Jennifer Lynn Stone (with son Oliver).

FRED SAVAGE

THEN Cute, confused Kevin Arnold.

NOW Less in front of the camera, more behind. After stints on sitcoms like *Working* and *Crumbs,* the Stanford alum graduated to directing episodes of Disney kid comedy *Phil of the Future,* Nickelodeon's *Drake & Josh* and the recently canceled CW comedy *Aliens in America,* as well as the 2007 film *Daddy Day Camp.* In 2004, Savage married Jennifer Lynn Stone, now 35; the pair had known each other as kids and reconnected years later at his birthday party. "We started talking and smooching, and we've been together ever since," says Savage, 32. Among their wedding vows: "I promised to always bring up a glass of water to her before we go to bed, and she promised to never let me dress myself." They have a son, Oliver, almost 2, and another child on the way.

"It went from 'Hey, aren't you Fred Savage's brother?' to 'Aren't you Scott Baio's friend?'" says Hervey (who appeared on Baio's show).

JASON HERVEY

THEN After 250 commercials and spots on shows like *Diff'rent Strokes,* he was immortalized as *Wonder*'s bullying older bro Wayne. "People expect me to come up and give them a wedgie," says Hervey. "They still love to hate Wayne."

NOW Hervey sold his first project, *Wide World of Kids,* at 17. "I wrote, produced and hosted it—and I've never looked back," says Hervey, a married dad of four. At 36, with his business partner Eric Bischoff, he produces celeb reality shows like the VH1 hit *Scott Baio Is 46 . . . and Pregnant.* "I was driving in the car, and it just hit me, 'Why haven't I created a show for Scott yet?' I'm pleased and humbled by how much people love the show," says Hervey, who has also created shows for Billy Rae Cyrus and Hulk Hogan.

BRIAN ROBBINS

THEN Played swoon-worthy tough guy Eric on the 1986-1991 classroom classic.

NOW After a brief stint hosting TV game show *Pictionary,* Brooklyn-born Robbins, 44, created kid comedies like Nickelodeon's *All That.* By 1997, he'd turned big-time producer-director on TV hits like *Smallville* and *One Tree Hill,* along with film fare like *Big Fat Liar* and *Norbit.*

Robbins produced *Wild Hogs* (2007, with Tim Allen); it took in more than $200 million worldwide.

In 2005, Cohen judged a "Truffle Shuffle" contest in Astoria, Ore. Max Reisfar, 11, who looks like a young Cohen, won.

THE GOONIES

JEFF COHEN

THEN Chunk, the pudgy kid who made the "Truffle Shuffle" dance famous in 1985's classic *The Goonies*.

NOW A successful entertainment lawyer in L.A. After *The Goonies*, Cohen, 34, did bit parts while following *Goonies'* director Richard Donner's advice to get an education. He attended UC Berkeley, where he was elected student body president (slogan: "Chunk for President") and, occasionally, by popular demand, did the Truffle Shuffle on the sidelines at football games. In a 2001 interview he stated that his "life goal is to be on an *A&E Biography* instead of an *E! True Hollywood Story*. . . . I have big plans."

I'm with the Band

Sometimes acting isn't enough. Sometimes casting directors aren't calling enough. Sometimes the urge just strikes. In each case, the remedy is often the same: Pick up a guitar and play

JARED LETO

Leto (see also page 18) fronting for his band 30 Seconds to Mars at San Francisco's Bill Graham Civic Auditorium in February '07.

JENNY LEWIS

THEN Fred Savage's runaway pal in the 198[...] age adventure movie *The Wizard*.

NOW Perhaps *the* breakout screen-to-mus[...] Lewis fronts the much-buzzed-about L.A[...] rock group Rilo Kiley. The band has release[...] albums, including the 2004 hit *More Advent[...]* and many of their songs have been heard on [...] like *Grey's Anatomy* and *Nip/Tuck*. Lewis, n[...] released the alt-country *Rabbit Fur Coat* in [...] PEOPLE's reviewer said she had "more sou[...] charm than you would expect any L.A. hips[...] have." A new solo album is in the works.

With Fred Savage and Luke Edwards in *The Wizard*, about a video-game championship.

BLOSSOM
JENNA VON OY

THEN Played fast-talking BFF Six on *Blossom* for four years.

NOW Settled since 2006 in Nashville, von Oy has gone country with her debut disc, *Breathing Room*, released last fall via her Web site www.jennavonoy.com. "It was crucial for me to have complete creative control," says the singer, who calls her sound "country-pop-soul-whatever. It's wholeheartedly me. I'm 31, and at this point, I don't want someone to mold me into something. I'm very confident in who I am." And while she's all about the music, von Oy hasn't forsaken her first love: TV. "I love comedy, the instant gratification of people getting a joke," says von Oy, most recently a regular on *The Parkers*.

"I hope they put *Blossom* on DVD," says von Oy (left), "because that's my childhood."

THE COSBY SHOW
MALCOLM-JAMAL WARNER

Malcolm-Jamal Warner (see also *The Cosby Show*, page 84) and his jazz/funk band, Miles Long, performed at Santa Monica's Temple Bar in September '06.

E.T.

HENRY THOMAS

THEN Elliot, *E.T.*'s 10-year-old protector.
NOW Thomas, 36, never strayed far from the screen—appearing in *Legends of the Fall* with Brad Pitt and Martin Scorsese's *Gangs of New York*—but he also got busy in the '90s as a rocker for a San Antonio band, the Blue Heelers. The band didn't survive a move to L.A., but Thomas continues to sing, play guitar and write songs.

In 1982's *E.T.*, Thomas befriends a stranded alien.

Pigeon worked up a sweat as a drummer.

FAMILY TIES

BRIAN BONSALL

THEN Tow-headed baby bro' Andy Keaton. **NOW** Bonsall retired from acting at 13, got pierced and tattooed and played in a punk band called Thruster. In 2004 he was arrested on suspicion of drunk driving and last August pulled two years probation for assaulting his girlfriend. Now 26, he completed a 30-day stint in rehab and works in construction in Colorado.

SILVER SPOONS

CORKY PIGEON

THEN Ricky Schroeder's geeky friend Freddy Lippincottleman on the '80s sitcom *Silver Spoons*. **NOW** Pigeon, 38, "did the punk rock thing" as a drummer with his Cali band, the Gain, but he's focused on acting again—and so is his daughter Taylor Nicole, 4. "No advice," says Dad. "But if she's not having fun, that's it."

LIFE GOES ON

CHRIS BURKE

THEN Corky Thacher on *Life Goes On*. "It was the first show of its kind on TV," says Burke of the 1989-93 run, on which he played a character with Down syndrome. "It changed the way people viewed Down syndrome, and I'm so proud to have been a part of it."
NOW Burke, 42, is the lead singer of his folk trio, the Chris Burke Band, which features brothers John and Joe DeMasi, whom he met at camp when he was 14. "We've been together for almost 25 years," says Burke of the band, which has released four albums and performs at school and charity events. "We're still going strong. I love it when we play the 'Oh Blah Di' theme from *Life Goes On*. The crowd just goes wild." Burke is still passionate about acting but devotes most of his time to serving as a goodwill ambassador for the National Down Syndrome Society. "I want to let people with Down syndrome know that they shouldn't give up. I want them to think, 'I can make a difference in people's lives,'" says the New York City resident, who leads the NDSS annual Buddy Walk.

The punk life, onstage and off; Bonsall's 2007 mugshot.

Back to Reality

From *The Surreal Life* to *Celebrity Fit Club*, *Celebrity Rehab* and *Celebrity Duets*, reality shows have given many former child actors a second shot at television

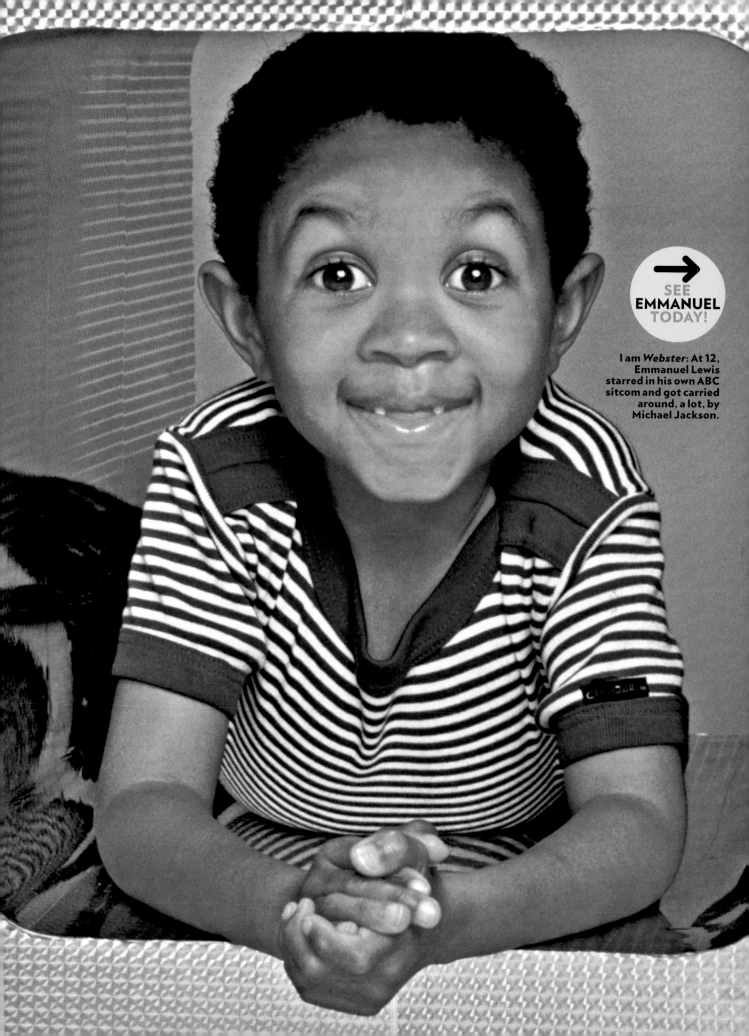

→ SEE EMMANUEL TODAY!

I am *Webster*: At 12, Emmanuel Lewis starred in his own ABC sitcom and got carried around, a lot, by Michael Jackson.

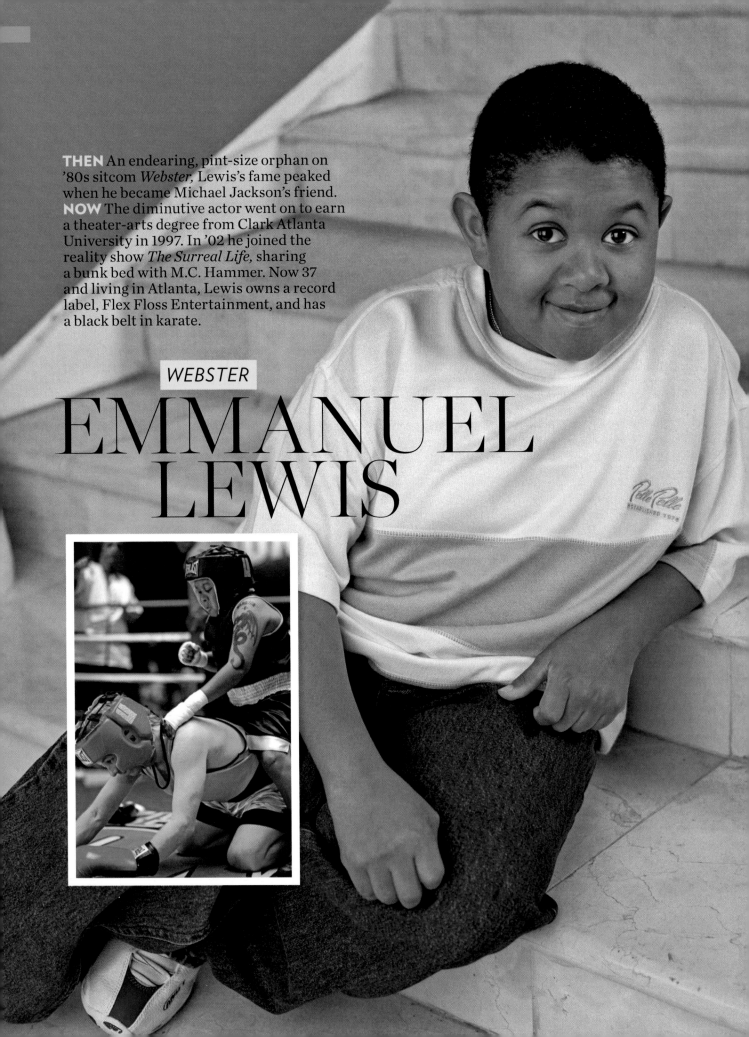

THEN An endearing, pint-size orphan on '80s sitcom *Webster,* Lewis's fame peaked when he became Michael Jackson's friend. **NOW** The diminutive actor went on to earn a theater-arts degree from Clark Atlanta University in 1997. In '02 he joined the reality show *The Surreal Life,* sharing a bunk bed with M.C. Hammer. Now 37 and living in Atlanta, Lewis owns a record label, Flex Floss Entertainment, and has a black belt in karate.

WEBSTER

EMMANUEL LEWIS

FAMILY TIES

TINA YOTHERS

▬

THEN Eye-rolling younger sibling Jennifer Keaton on the mid-'80s sitcom *Family Ties*.

NOW Real life: After trying her hand at the music biz, Yothers, 34, married contractor Robert Kaiser in 2002 and had daughter Lillian, 2, and son Jake, 9 months. In 2006 she was back in the news as reigning champ on *Celebrity Fit Club* and returned to the show after giving birth in the fall.

Yothers smiles with her children Lillian and Jake; during her *Family Ties* years; and with the members of her band Jaded (in 2000).

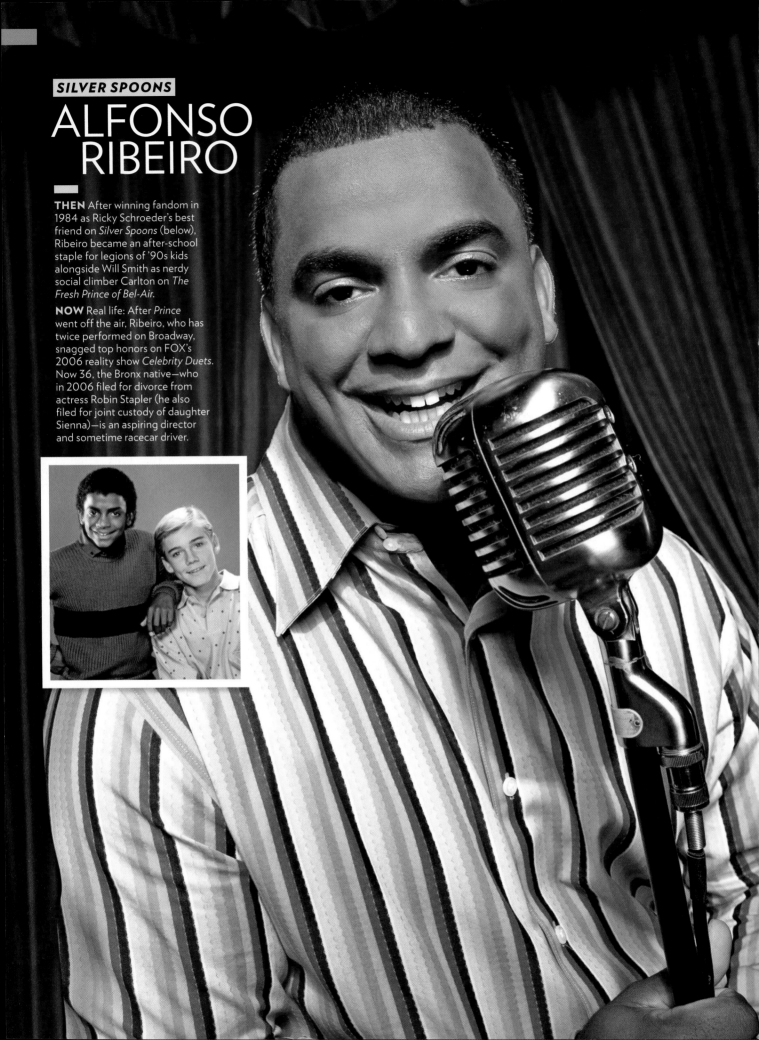

ALFONSO RIBEIRO

THEN After winning fandom in 1984 as Ricky Schroeder's best friend on *Silver Spoons* (below), Ribeiro became an after-school staple for legions of '90s kids alongside Will Smith as nerdy social climber Carlton on *The Fresh Prince of Bel-Air*.

NOW Real life: After *Prince* went off the air, Ribeiro, who has twice performed on Broadway, snagged top honors on FOX's 2006 reality show *Celebrity Duets*. Now 36, the Bronx native—who in 2006 filed for divorce from actress Robin Stapler (he also filed for joint custody of daughter Sienna)—is an aspiring director and sometime racecar driver.

THE LOST BOYS

COREY HAIM & COREY FELDMAN

THEN Vampire chasers in 1987's comedy-horror film *The Lost Boys.* **NOW** Haim scored a string of flicks in the '80s—including three with tween idol Feldman—but his career dive-bombed after too many B-movies and a drug problem. He filed for bankruptcy in 1997 and reportedly tried to sell one of his teeth on eBay in 2001. Now clean and sober, Haim, 36, re-upped with Feldman in A&E's "scripted reality" show *The Two Coreys,* now entering its second season. The Coreys will also reprise their *Lost Boys* roles in the sequel *Lost Boys: The Tribe,* slated for a July release.

"It was almost like Beatlemania," Feldman, left, in 1989 with frequent costar Haim, said of the pair's '80s popularity.

MAUREEN McCORMICK

THE BRADY BUNCH

CHRISTOPHER KNIGHT

THEN Peter, mischievous middle son on *The Brady Bunch*.

NOW Though never disowning his Brady-ness—Manhattan-born Knight has appeared in numerous reunion films and TV shows after the original 1969-1974 series—he has also had a successful run as a high-tech entrepreneur, marketing interactive kids' products and an Internet casting network. In 2005 Knight, 50, appeared on VH1's *The Surreal Life*, where he met Adrianne Curry, 25, winner of the first *America's Next Top Model*. The beauty and the geek ("Opposites can actually work together," Knight has said) chronicled their romance, nuptials and subsequent marriage counseling on VH1's *My Fair Brady*.

THEN Everyone's favorite big sister, Marcia Brady.

NOW After *The Brady Bunch* wrapped in 1974, McCormick began a decadelong struggle with bulimia and cocaine. Her life stabilized in 1985 when she married printer salesman Michael Cummings; they had a daughter, Natalie, four years later. Though she did many guest spots over the years, it wasn't until 2007 that McCormick, 51, again became a TV regular, joining VH1's *Celebrity Fit Club* after gaining 30 lbs. A talented singer since her *Brady* days, McCormick recorded a well-received country album, *When You Get a Little Lonely,* in 1995 and appeared this year on CMT's *Gone Country* (above), a celebrity competition to find the next country superstar. Her autobiography, *Here's the Story,* is set for an October release, and she promises a frank and hopeful account of her "demons" and "tumultuous storms."

Greg, Cindy and Bobby Brady (Barry Williams, Susan Olsen and Mike Lookinland, that is) attended Knight and Curry's 2006 wedding.

Foxworth, right, on *Matters*, before her character was abruptly cut in '93; above, in the January '08 premiere of *Rehab*.

JAIMEE FOXWORTH

THEN Judy Winslow, winsome baby sister on *Family Matters*.

NOW On the fourth season of that early '90s hit, cute Judy Winslow climbed the living room stairs to her room and was never heard from again. Budget concerns were behind the decision, but 13-year-old Winslow was crushed. Later she battled alcoholism and depression. She returned to the public eye as a 19-year-old star of a porn film that was soon plastered across the Internet—an error in judgment she discussed on a 2006 *Oprah* episode titled "Former Child TV Star Reveals the Biggest Mistake of Her Life." Nearly two years later, Foxworth, 28, appeared on VH1's reality show *Celebrity Rehab with Dr. Drew*, where she sought help for marijuana addiction.

Bledsoe with Bill Cosby and, below, on *Fit Club*.

THEN As *Cosby* kid Vanessa, she perfected the petulant fourth child.
NOW After tackling the topic of weight on her short-lived, self-titled talk show from 1995-96, Bledsoe, 34, turned to the VH1 reality show *Celebrity Fit Club* for more help slimming down in 2006. "I've always worked out, but I thought the opportunity to focus on it solely for 100 days would be really good," Bledsoe, who keeps to a vegetarian diet, said about her reasons for appearing on the show. Her only regret? Giving up ginger ale: "I love it to death." The actress most recently appeared in the Oxygen TV movie *Husband for Hire* with Mark Consuelos and Erik Estrada.

TEMPESTT BLEDSOE

THE COSBY SHOW

Gone too soon

When child stars die, drugs, and sometimes despair, often play a role

River Phoenix (below right, with, from left, Wil Wheaton, Jerry O'Connell and Corey Feldman) was 14 when he made *Stand by Me*. He died nine years later.

RIVER PHOENIX

1970–1993

He was a cute kid in *Stand by Me* and a convincingly angst-ridden teen in darker fare like *Running on Empty* and *My Own Private Idaho.* On Oct. 31, 1993, he became, for a generation, a symbol of everything that could go wrong for a young actor in Hollywood when he collapsed, thrashing spasmodically, on the sidewalk outside L.A.'s Viper Club. Phoenix, 23, died within an hour of heart failure; an autopsy later cited "multiple drug intoxication" as the cause.

Phoenix's death shocked many who thought they knew him well but had been unaware of his drug use. But River himself had admitted to keeping things hidden— to having "chameleon qualities"—and had also once noted, in response to *Stand by Me* costar Corey Feldman's arrest for heroin possession, that drug users weren't always obvious. "Drugs aren't just done by bad guys and sleazebags," he said. "It's a universal disease."

In 1996 Renfro was cast in the Barry Levinson film *Sleepers.*

BRAD RENFRO

1982–2008

The first time he was busted—at age 15, for possessing cocaine and marijuana—actor Brad Renfro said he learned a lesson about taking drugs. "If you've never done it, don't," Renfro, who made more than 20 movies and struck many as a special talent, told PEOPLE after his 1998 arrest. "If you have done it, pray."

Tragically, drugs remained part of his life. On Jan. 15 friends found Renfro dead in bed in an L.A. apartment after a night of drinking. The friends heard Renfro snoring early that morning, but when they checked on him shortly before 9 a.m., he wasn't breathing. An autopsy determined the 25-year-old actor had died from an accidental heroin overdose.

Raised in Knoxville, Tenn., Renfro was just 10 when picked to play a gutsy witness in a Mafia case in 1994's *The Client*; the next year he won *The Hollywood Reporter*'s Young Star Award. In recent months Renfro, who had just wrapped a part alongside Billy Bob Thornton in the drama *The Informers*, "had been working hard and was very focused on the future," says his attorney Richard Kaplan. "He was a really good, warm person. I don't think he had a bad bone in his body."

SEAQUEST DSV

JONATHAN BRANDIS

1976–2003

Best known for his starring roles in the film *The Neverending Story II* and Steven Spielberg's futuristic science fiction series *seaQuest DSV*, Brandis later had difficulty re-creating that level of success. On Nov. 11, 2003, the 27-year-old actor hanged himself in his Los Angeles apartment building and died the next day. Friends told PEOPLE he had been despondent about the state of his career and had become a heavy drinker.

DIFF'RENT STROKES

DANA PLATO

1964–1999

A charming kid on the hit sitcom *Diff'rent Strokes,* Dana Plato may be almost as well remembered for the sad, slow-motion plane wreck of her career. Plato started on *Strokes* at 13, and, according to her manager, overdosed on Valium at 14; by 15 she was coming to the set drunk; at 18 she became pregnant and was dropped from the show (custody was later awarded to the father).

A few years later, short of cash, she famously robbed a Las Vegas video store of $164 while brandishing a pellet gun ("I've just been robbed by the girl who played Kimberly on *Diff'rent Strokes,*" the clerk told the 911 operator). Somewhere along the way she was arrested for forging Valium prescriptions, posed nude for *Playboy* and appeared in a soft-core porn flick, *Different Strokes: The story of Jack and Jill . . . and Jill.*

On May 7, 1999, Plato, 34, appeared on Howard Stern's radio show, where her history prompted a number of cruel jokes. The next day, her boyfriend found her unconscious; the medical examiner later ruled her death—from an overdose of a powerful pain reliever—a suicide.

Plato, says her cousin Kim Jaafil, was "always an outgoing, bubbly kid, very happy and well-adjusted."

After O'Rourke died, MGM used a body double stand-in to complete her part in *Poltergeist III.*

POLTERGEIST

HEATHER O'ROURKE

1975–1988

The sweet, spooky kid in *Poltergeist* who first uttered the film's memorable tag line, "They're here," Heather O'Rourke, 12, woke up on a February morning in 1988 with what seemed to be flu-like symptoms. Her condition quickly worsened; hours later, she was airlifted to a San Diego hospital, where she was operated on for intestinal stenosis, an acute bowel obstruction—a congenital condition neither her mother nor stepfather had suspected. She died on the operating table.

I'M NOT A KID,
BUT I PLAYED ONE ON TV!

Some young stars had a not-so-surprising secret: After a hard day on the set, they were old enough—legally—to take the edge off with a double martini

BEVERLY HILLS, 90210

"I'm 24!"
—LUKE PERRY

"21!"
—JASON PRIESTLEY

"29!"
—GABRIELLE CARTERIS

CLUELESS

SIXTEEN CANDLES

"I'm 24!"
—ELISA DONOVAN

"I was 17 —12 years ago!"
—STACEY DASH, AS ONE OF *CLUELESS*'S HIGH SCHOOL ALPHA GIRLS

"I'm 29!"
—GEDDE WATANABE, HIGH SCHOOL EXCHANGE STUDENT

"Actually, I was the Karate 23-year-old!"
—*THE KARATE KID*'S RALPH MACCHIO

THE KARATE KID

DOOGIE HOWSER

"I'm 22!"
—*DOOGIE HOWSER*'S MAX CASELLA (WITH NEIL PATRICK HARRIS)

INDEX

MASTHEAD

Editor Cutler Durkee **Creative Director** Sara Williams **Director of Photography** Chris Dougherty **Art Director** Cass Spencer **Photography Editor** C. Tiffany Lee Ramos **Editorial Manager** Daniel S. Levy **Designer** Eulie Lee **Writers** Sona Charaipotra, Kara Warner, Danielle Anderson, Debra Lewis-Boothman, Molly Lopez, Kristen Mascia, Ellen Shapiro, Larry Sutton **Reporters** David Chiu, Ivory Jeff Clinton, Deirdre Gallagher, Lucy Hitz, Lesley Messer, Hugh McCarten, Vincent R. Peterson, Thailan Pham, Jane Sugden, Emmet Sullivan, Christina Tapper, Shari Weiss, Melody Wells **Copy Editors** Ben Harte (Chief) James Bradley, Aura Davies, Lance Kaplan, Alan Levine, Jennifer Shotz **Production Editors** Denise M. Doran, Cynthia Miele, Daniel J. Neuburger **Scanners** Brien Foy, Stephen Pabarue **Imaging** Romeo Cifelli, Jeff Ingledue and Robert Roszkowski **Special thanks to** Robert Britton, David Barbee, Jane Bealer, Sal Covarrúbias, Margery Frohlinger, Suzy Im, Ean Sheehy, Jack Styczynski, Céline Wojtala, Patrick Yang

TIME INC. HOME ENTERTAINMENT
Publisher Richard Fraiman, **General Manager** Steven Sandonato, **Executive Director Marketing Services** Carol Pittard, **Director Retail & Special Sales** Tom Mifsud, **Director New Product Development** Peter Harper, **Assistant Director Brand Marketing** Laura Adam, **Associate Counsel** Helen Wan, **Senior Brand Manager** TWRS/M, Holly Oakes, **Book Production Manager** Suzanne Janso, **Design & Prepress Manager** Anne-Michelle Gallero **Special thanks to** Glenn Buonocore, Susan Chodakiewicz, Margaret Hess, Dennis Marcel, Robert Marasco, Brooke Reger, Mary Sarro-Waite, Ilene Schreider, Adriana Tierno, Alex Voznesenskiy

ISBN 10: 1-60320-014-2   **ISBN 13:** 978-1-60320-014-1
Library of Congress Number: 2008903220

CREDITS

FRONT COVER
(clockwise from top right) Al Levine/NBCU Photo Bank; Everett; Foto Fantasies; ABC Photo Archives; Reuters; Everett; Globe

CONTENTS
2 (clockwise from top left) MPTV; Photofest; Screen Scenes (2); 3 Everett (2)

DREAMBOATS
4 (from left) Everett (3); Dave Bjerke/NBCU Photo Bank; 5 Everett; 6 Photograph by Michael Murphree; Styling by Lorraine Hobler/Zenobia; Grooming by Heather Hawkins/Zenobia; 8-9 (clockwise from right) Michael Murphree (3); Courtesy Christopher Atkins; 10 Globe; 11 (from top) Courtesy Kirk Cameron; ABC Photo Archives; 12 (clockwise from right) Courtesy Kirk Cameron (2); Todd Stone; 13 Everett; (inset) Sven Hoogerhuis/LFI; 14 (from top) Jonathan Friolo/Splash News; Photofest; 15 Marcel Hartmann/Corbis; (insets from left) Kobal; Photofest; 16 Greg Gorman; 17 Photofest; 18 Justin Stephens/Corbis; (insets from left) Mark Selinger/ABC Photo Archives; Cau-Guerin/Abaca USA; 19 Erin Patrice O'Brien/Corbis; 20 Michael Sharkey; (insets from left) Everett (2); 21 (clockwise from top left) Everett (2); Lucas Jackson/Reuters; 22 David Gabber/PR Photos; 23 Kobal; 24 (from top) Chris Weeks/Wireimage; MPTV; 25 Danielle Levitt/August Images; (inset) ABC Photo Archives

SECOND LIFE
26 (from left) Kobal; Photofest; Foto Fantasies; NBCU Photo Bank; 27 Everett/Rex USA; 28-29 (clockwise from left) Danielle Levitt/August Images (2); Foto Fantasies; Tonya Wise/London Entertainment/Splash News; 30 (from top) Everett; Kobal; 31 Peter Serling; 32 (from top) Danielle Levitt/August Images; ABC Photo Archives; Chris Haston; Courtesy Eve Plumb; 33 MPTV; 34 (clockwise from top left) Christopher Ameruso; ABC Photo Archives; Everett; MPTV; 35 Courtesy Kellie Williams (2); 36 Wayne Schoenfeld; (insets from left) Courtesy Amy O'Neill; Everett; 38 (from top) Christa Renee; Courtesy The Little Seed (2); 39 Gary NUII/NBCU Photo Bank; 40 (from top) ABC Photo Archives; Maia Madison; 41 (from top) Photofest; Courtesy Ilan Mitchell Smith; 42 Everett; 43 (from top) Richard Austin/Rex USA; Courtesy Quay Studios; Stephanie Hogue; 44 Everett; (insets from top) Photofest; Courtesy Charlie Korsmo; 45 Courtesy Taran Noah Smith (2); (inset) Everett; 46 (from top) MPTV; Howard Wise/JPI; 47 (clockwise from bottom right) Michael O'Connor; Courtesy Ariana Richards (2); Photofest

BIG STARS
48 (from left) Everett; Kobal; Globe; CBS/Landov; 49 Kobal; 50-51 James Devaney/Wireimage; 52-53 (from left) Kobal; Michael Tran/Filmmagic; Kobal; 54 Mario Casilli/MPTV; (inset) Jeffrey Mayer/Wireimage; 55 (clockwise from top left) Bill Davila/Startraks; Gilbert Flores/Celebrity Photo; Brian Zak/Gamma; Ronald Asadorian/Splash; CBS/Landov; 56 David James/Warner Bros; (inset) Kobal; 57 Kobal; (inset) Matt Sayles/AP; 58 Kobal; (inset) Mike Marsland/INF; 59 (clockwise from top) Photofest; Everett; Jemal Countess/Wireimage; Shooting Star; 60 Cliff Lipson/CBS/Landov (inset) Christina Radish/LFI; 61 Chris Polk/Filmmagic; 62 Eric Charbonneau/Wireimage; (insets from left) Shooting Star; Photofest; 63 Don Flood; (inset) Kobal; 64 (clockwise from bottom right) Stephen Danelian (2); CBS/Landov; 65 Everett; (insets from left) Everett; Splash; 66 (clockwise from top) New Line Cinema;

MPTV; Everett; 67 Todd Williamson/Wireimage; (inset) Photofest; 68 Kobal; (insets from top) Globe; INF; 69 Kobal; (insets from left) Kobal; Ray Williams/TLP; 70-71 Armando Gallo/Retna; (inset) ABC Photo Archives; 72 Jade Albert (insets from left) Frank Micelotta/Wireimage; Sunset Photo & News; 73 Everett; (inset) Ronald Asadorian/Splash; 74 Michael Wilfing/Vanit/Retna; (inset) from top) Paul Hiffmeyer/AP; Everett; Jay Brady/Everett; Don Watson/ABC Photo Archives; 76 (clockwise from top) Melissa Moseley/Columbia Pictures; JD-KO/Flynet; Martha Noble/Globe; 77 Armando Gallo/Retna

IN THE GAME
78 (from left) ABC Photo Archives; Everett; Chris Haston/NBCU Photo Bank; MPTV; 79 Kathy Hutchins/Hutchins; (inset) Globe; 80 (from top) Amy Graves/Wireimage; Michael Tran/Filmmagic; Michael Tammaro/Retna; Alison Dyer; 81 Photofest; 82 Danielle Levitt/August Images; (inset) Foto Fantasies; 83 (from top) Zuma; Adam Nemser/Photolink; 84 NBCU Photo Bank; (inset) Al Levine/NBCU Photo Bank; 85 (clockwise from top left) Fred Prouser/Reuters; Sthanlee B. Mirador/Shooting Star; Jeff Kravitz/Filmmagic; L Martinez/AFF-USA; Erin Patrice O'Brien; 86 Courtesy Josie Davis; 87 Stewart Volland/Retna; (inset) Photofest; 88 (clockwise from top left) John Elliott/Hutchins; NBCU Photo Bank; Gregory Pace/BEImages; Giulio Marcocchi/SIPA; 89 (clockwise from top) Everett; Steve Buckley/Buzzfoto; Denise Truscello/Wireimage; Apega/Abaca USA; 90 ABC Photo Archives (inset) Malcolm Ali/Wireimage; 91 (from top) Photofest; Kimberly White/Reuters; Screen Scenes; Courtesy Aileen Quinn; 92 Everett; 93

(from top) Patrick Rideaux/Rex USA; Paul Mounce/Corbis; Courtesy Michael Fishman; 94 (from top) Courtesy Pepsi Co.; Carley Margolis/Filmmagic; Ciao Hollywood/Splash; Mario Casilli/MPTV; 95 Danielle Levitt/August Images; (insets) Chris Haston/NBCU Photo Bank (2); 96 (from top) Marc Royce; MPTV; Screen Scenes; 97 Amy & Stuart Photography; 98 Emma Bass (2); 99 Everett; 100 (clockwise from top) Photofest; Everett; Photofest; Scott Wintrow/Getty; 101 (clockwise from left) Kobal; Jill Ann Spaulding/Filmmagic; Kobal; 102 New Line Cinema; (inset) Michael Caulfield/Wireimage; 103 (from top) Marc Royce/Corbis Outline; Everett; 104 (clockwise from right) Robert Mora/Wireimage; Kobal (2); Courtesy Gaby Hoffmann (2); 105 Shooting Star; (inset) Bryce Duffy/Corbis Outline; 106 Dennis Kleiman/Retna; 107 (from top) Kobal; Everett

VOICE-OVER
108 Warner Bros; (inset) Radial Press; 109 (clockwise from top) The CW; MPTV (2); Vaughn Youtz/Zuma; 110 (clockwise from top) Courtesy Burning Man; Warner Bos. (2); Courtesy Alexander Polinsky (2); Photofest; 111 (clockwise from top) Courtesy Disney; David Lee/Vistalux; Everett (2)

IN THE BIZ
112 (from left) ABC Photo Archives (2); Everett; MPTV; 113 Foto Fantasies; 114 Bryon Purvis/Admedia; (inset) Courtesy Universal; 115 (from top) Photofest; Courtesy Drama 34; 116 Marc Royce; (inset) ABC Photo Archives; 117 (clockwise from top) Susie Ramos/Sony Pictures; MPTV; SIPA; Alberto Rodriguez/Getty Images for Fox; 118-119 MPTV; (insets) The Daily Astorian (2)

BAND
121 Rune Hellestad/Corbis; 122 Jason Kempin/Filmmagic;

(inset) Photofest; 122 (clockwise from top) Photofest; Brandi Pettijohn/Filmmagic; Courtesy Jenna Von Oy; Brooke Ludwick; 124 Jeff Vespa/Wireimage; (insets from left) Courtesy Henry Thomas; Shooting Star; 125 (from top) Courtesy Corky Pigeon; Frank Carroll/NBCU Photo Bank; Courtesy Corky Pigeon; Richard M. Hackett/Longmont Daily Times/Zuma; Coulder County Colorado Sheriff's Dept./The Daily Camera/AP; Christopher Voelker/Shooting Star

REALITY
126 (from left) MPTV; Bud Gray/MPTV; Everett; ABC Photo Archives; 127 Everett; 128 Photofest; Courtesy Paramount; 129 (clockwise from top) Gilles Mingasson/VH1; Lisa Rose/JPI; Beth Herzhaft; Herb Ball/NBCU Photo Bank; 130 Everett; (inset) MPTV; 131 (from left) Everett; Andrew Eccles/A&E; 132 MPTV; 133 (from top) MPTV; Ron Jaffe/CMT; VH1; 134 (from top) Evans Ward/VH1; ABC Photo Archives; Mario Casilli/MPTV; VH1; 135 VH1

GONE TOO SOON
137 Photofest; 138 Ron Brown/Corbis; 139 (from top) Kevin Winter/Getty; Screen Scenes; 140 Lynn Goldsmith/Corbis; (inset) Aaron Rapoport/MPTV; 141 (from top) Pacha/Corbis; Herb Ball/NBCU Photo Bank; Kobal

TOO OLD
142 (clockwise from top left) MPTV; Corbis; Globe; Everett; Photofest; Everett; MPTV; Everett; 143 Everett (3)

BACK COVER
(clockwise from top right) Paul Hawthorne/Startraks; Stewart Cook/Rex USA; Andreas Branch/PMC/SIPA; Byron Purvis/Admedia/SIPA; RAMEY; Lawrence Lucier/Filmmagic; Scott Kirkland/Globe

HICKMANS